Stories of Great
African Americans

Additional Series in the
**Forgotten Classics
Family Library**

World History Series

Freedom Series

Story Hour Series

Nature, Art and Music Series

Stories of
Great
African
Americans

By Selected Authors

FORGOTTEN CLASSICS FAMILY LIBRARY
Libraries of Hope

Stories of Great African Americans

Unsung Heroes, by Elizabeth Ross Haynes, New York: DuBois and Dill, Publishers, (1921).

The Upward Path, A Reader for Colored Children, by Myron T. Pritchard and Mary White Ovington, New York: Harcourt, Brace and Howe, (1920).

Finding a Way Out, by Robert Moton, New York: Doubleday, Page & Company, (1920).

Cover image credit: The Lord Is My Shepherd, by Eastman Johnson, 1863. Smitsonian American Art Museum, Gift of Mrs. Francis P. Garvin, from Wikimedia Commons.

Libraries of Hope, Inc.
Appomattox, Virginia 24522

Website www.librariesofhope.com
Email support@librariesofhope.com

Printed in the United States of America

Table of Contents

Frederick Douglass ...... *Middle School* 1
How I Escaped ...... *Best read after, But older - 8m?* 30

Paul Laurence Dunbar 39

The Boy and the Bayonet 59

Booker Taliaferro Washington 73

Up from Slavery 95

Harriet Tubman 101

Blanche Kelso Bruce 117

Benjamin Banneker 125

Benjamin Banneker 137

Phillis Wheatley 140

Josiah Henson 151

Sojourner Truth 168

Crispus Attucks 187

Paul Cuffé 194

Paul Cuffé 205

Alexander Crummell 212

John Mercer Langston 216

Introduction 227

Going to School Under Difficulties 231

The Beginnings of a Mississippi School 237

My First School 239

The Colored Cadet at West Point 250

A Negro Explorer at the North Pole 256

Table of Contents Continued

Matthew A. Henson..................................256

Negro Music That Stirred France 264

How Two Colored Captains Fell.........................272

Ira Aldridge...274

Out of Africa...279

Oath of Afro-American Youth 291

The Negro Race...292

A Mere Matter of the Feelings.............................293

Frederick Douglass

The Orator and Abolitionist
1817-1895

Tuckahoe is the name of a plantation on the eastern shore of Maryland. It was once known for its worn-out, flat, sandy soil; for its old, poorly-kept fields and fences, and for its uneducated and ignorant people. On one side of this plantation flowed a lazy, muddy river, bringing with it, as some believed, ague and fever.

At some distance from the river bank stood rows of log cabins suggestive of a quaint village whose only streets are the trodden footpaths and whose only street lights are the moon and the stars.

The cabins all looked very much alike except one which stood off to itself. Each one of these cabins had a door but no window, a dirt floor, a fence-rail loft for a bed, and a ladder by which to reach it. And each had a clay chimney with a broad open fireplace and just a block of wood at the door for steps. In this little log-cabin village, called "the quarters" lived the slaves.

Nearly every morning, just at peep of day, the cabin doors were unfastened and people began to stir until "the quarters" were almost like a beehive. Men, women, and children large enough to work were getting ready to go to the fields nearby. Some with their smoking clay or corn-cob pipes in their mouths were jumping astride the bare backs of mules or horses. Some were beginning to ride off without a sound other than that of the jingle of gear and the beat of hoofs. Still others followed.

Now and then a woman hastened to the lone cabin which stood off from "the quarters", pulling by the hand a child or two, or carrying them in her arms. She tarried at this cabin, presided over by "Grandma" Betsy Bailey, just long enough to leave her little children and then hastened on to the field.

Grandma Betsy, an active old fisherwoman, fed the children just as a man feeds his pigs. After placing the mush in a little trough, she set the trough either down on the dirt floor or out in the yard. Then she waved her hand to the children, who made a rush for the trough, each with a little piece of board or an oyster shell in his hand for a spoon. Some of them, without seeming to rush, tried to eat faster than the others, but Aunt Betsy had only to cut a sharp eye at such offenders.

She never thought of trying to call any one of them by name except her own grandson, Frederick Augustus Washington Bailey. Children on the Tuckahoe plantation were not supposed to have names or to know about their ages. Neither were they supposed to know the names of the days of the week or the months of the year, or to know anything at all about time.

Frederick thought much of Grandma Betsy's cabin, of the eating trough, of his bed in the loft by her side, and of the potato hole in front of her cabin fireplace. Little thought of his age or of any separation from his grandma ever entered his mind. Grandma Betsy, however, spent a part of each day thinking especially of his age and the time when he would be separated from her.

She had already begun to picture the circumstances of their separation. One day she said to herself as she sat patting her foot: "Freddie is just about seven years old now. I know old Master will soon be sending someone down from the 'Great House' for him". She waited and looked and listened for days but no one came. She was beginning to wonder where old Master was, when suddenly one Friday afternoon he came down himself and gave orders for Frederick to be carried away the next day. Grandma Betsy simply curtsied, saying, "Yes sir, Master, yes sir".

On this particular afternoon she was engaged in mending her net for fishing. She finished her task at the close of the day, and early that night she climbed the ladder leading to the bed in the loft of the cabin with tears trickling down her cheeks. She lay down on her bed by the side of Frederick, but instead of going to sleep she lay there thinking, thinking, thinking. Finally the comforting words of an old plantation melody came to her mind. She began singing it to herself just above a whisper:

A little talk with Jesus makes it right, all right.
A little talk with Jesus makes it right, all right.
   Troubles of every kind—
   Thank God, we always find
A little talk with Jesus makes it right.

Over and over again she sang it until she dozed off into a light slumber. Suddenly the straws on her rail bed seemed to stick her and the hard rails seemed to push up through the rags and hurt her sides. She turned and twisted and opened her eyes, but refused to admit to herself that she was restless until again she began to sing over and over the melody:

A little talk with Jesus makes it right, all right.

The singing finally died away and all was quiet.

The next morning Grandma Betsy rose even earlier than usual and went about her work. Frederick also soon tumbled down from the loft without any thought of a bath or of changing his shirt, for, like the other slave boys, he dressed just once a week and that was Saturday night when he took his bath.

On this Saturday morning Grandma Betsy turned about more rapidly than usual and was therefore soon ready to start on her journey. With a white cloth on her head tied in turban style and the stem of her clay pipe between her teeth, she walked out, pulled and fastened the door behind her and stretched out her hand to Frederick who was sitting on the door-step. "Come, Freddie, we are going away today", said she.

He looked at her and asked, "Where are we going, Grandma?"

She simply shook her head, saying again, "Come on son".

Accustomed to obeying, he arose and grasped her hand but seemingly more reluctantly than usual. Out they went.

After a time Frederick began to stumble along as the journey lengthened, murmuring, "I am tired, Grandma."

Grandma Betsy stopped and squatted down. "Get on my shoulders, son", she said. Freddie stepped behind her, placed his little arms around her neck and with her assistance scrambled up on her shoulders with his legs about her neck. Not another word was spoken. Grandma Betsy rose with her burden and trudged on until Freddie begged her to let him walk again so that she might rest. Finally she squatted down, and Freddie with his tired little limbs almost fell off her shoulders.

Grandma Betsy stretched out both her arms. "Whew!" she said.

Freddie looked at her then and placed his arms around her as best he could, saying tenderly, "Grandma Betsy, was I heavy? Are you tired? I am so sorry".

They continued the journey until they reached the home of Frederick's new master on a plantation twelve miles away. Immediately they went into the kitchen where there were children of all colors, besides Aunt Katie, the cook. The children asked Frederick to come out and play with them but he refused until his grandmother urged him to go. They went out behind the kitchen. Frederick stood around at first as if afraid of the other children. Then he backed up against the kitchen wall and stood there as if he thought the kitchen might run away from him. While he stood there Grandma Betsy tip-toed out unseen by him.

One of the children came up to him and said, "Fred, Fred, your grandma's gone!" Frederick ran into the house as fast as he could and looked all around for her. Not seeing her, he ran a little way down the road and called her. She did not answer. Then he fell down and began to kick and cry. His brother and two sisters who had formerly been brought there tried to pet him, and to coax him to eat some apples and pears.

"No", said he, still kicking, "I want Grandma". There he lay until nightfall, when Aunt Katie came out and told him he must come in. He went in and lay down in the corner, crying and begging to be taken back home. The trip that day, however, had made him so tired that he soon fell asleep.

The next morning he asked Aunt Katie when Grandma Betsy was coming back to get him. She rolled her eyes and cast such fiery glances at him that Frederick understood and hushed. He had thought of asking for ash-cake like that which Grandma Betsy used to make, but her look drove that out of his mind.

Aunt Katie was not long in giving Frederick to understand that he was to drive up the cows every evening, keep the yard clean, and wait on Miss Lucretia, his master's daughter. The very first time Frederick went on an errand for Miss Lucretia she smiled and gave him a piece of buttered bread. He smiled, too, from ear to ear, bowed and ran off eating and wondering how she knew that he was so hungry. He always ran smiling whenever she called him. And when hunger pinched his little stomach hard, he nearly always crept under Miss Lucretia's window and tried to sing like Grandma Betsy:

A little talk with Jesus makes it right, all right.
A little talk with Jesus makes it right, all right.

He knew the next line but scarcely ever had chance to sing it before the window was opened and a piece of buttered bread was handed out to him.

One evening during his first summer on this plantation the rain poured down seemingly in sheets. He could not stand under the window and try to sing and he had in some way offended Aunt Katie. She stood at the kitchen table cutting bread for the other children and occasionally brandishing the knife at Frederick, saying, "I'll starve you, sir". He sat there watching the other children eat, watching Aunt Katie and still keeping one eye on an ear of corn on the shelf by the fire place. He did not lose his first opportunity to seize it and slip a few grains off the cob into the fire to parch.

While he sat there easing the parched grains of corn into his mouth, to his great joy in walked his own mother with a few cakes for him. She caressed him and asked him several questions. Seeing how nearly starved he was, she shook her fist at Aunt Katie and laid down the law to her. Then she tarried with her child for the last time, and even then just a short while—for she knew that she must again walk the twelve miles back to her home before the overseers came out and the horn was blown for field time.

Aunt Katie, remembering that stormy evening with Frederick's mother, said to him one day, "Come, Fred, and get a piece of bread. Dip it into this pot liquor". He curtsied first, then eagerly taking the bread, he walked up to the pot and dipped it and his hand as well into the greasy broth. For a few minutes he looked as though he would eat both bread and hand but the rattling of the dishes in his master's dining-room attracted his attention. He hesitated a moment, then smacked his greasy lips and bowed himself out of the kitchen and around to the side door of the dining-room.

Just as he reached the door of the dining-room, a big, grey cat slid in. Frederick slid in too. Immediately they began to scramble for the crumbs under the table. As soon as these were gobbled up, Frederick rushed into the yard to get some of the bones and scraps which the maid had just thrown out for "Nep", the dog.

Clad, winter and summer, in just a tow sack shirt scarcely reaching to his knees, Frederick was as scantily clothed as he was fed. On cold winter days he often stood on the sunny side of the house or in the chimney corner to keep warm. On cold nights he crept into the kitchen closet and got into the meal bag headforemost. In addition to these hardships, he often saw his own relatives and others cruelly beaten. Burdened with such experiences, his childish heart began to long for another place to live.

One day, while he was in this unhappy frame of mind, Miss Lucretia called him, saying that within three days he would be sent to Baltimore, to live for a while with her brother and sister, Mr. and Mrs. Hugh Auld. "You must go to the creek and wash all the dead skin off of your feet and knees," she said to him. "The people in Baltimore are clean. They will laugh at you if you look dirty. You cannot put on pants unless you get all the dirt off," she added. Frederick made himself busy, spending most of the three days in the creek, and part of the three nights jumping up to see if the boat was ready to go.

The following Saturday morning early, the boat sailed out of the Miles River for Baltimore. It was loaded with a flock of sheep for the market, and a few passengers, among whom was Frederick. After giving the old plantation a last look, as he thought, he made his way to the bow of the boat and spent the remainder of the day looking ahead. They arrived in Baltimore on Sunday morning. After Frederick had assisted in driving the sheep to the slaughter-house, one of the boat hands went with him to the home of Mr. and Mrs. Auld.

Mr. and Mrs. Auld and their little son, Thomas, met Frederick at the door and greeted him heartily. "Here is your Freddie who will take care of you, Tommy. Freddie, you must be kind to little Tommy", said Mrs. Auld. Frederick smiled and nodded his head. Thomas at once took hold of Frederick's hand and seemingly wished to hurry him into the house to see his toys.

The children played until they heard Mrs. Auld begin to read. Frederick stopped playing to listen. Thomas said, "Oh, come on, Freddie, let's play. That is just Mother reading the Bible. She reads it that way every day when Father is away".

"The Bible? What is that?" asked Frederick, looking at Thomas. Little Thomas, surprised because Frederick had never seen a Bible, ushered him into the room where his mother was reading. Thomas knew better than to interrupt his mother while she was reading, but as soon as she stopped, he told her why he had brought Frederick in. Mrs. Auld showed him the Bible, asked him a few questions and sent them both out to play.

Days passed, but not one when Mrs. Auld failed to read her Bible. Frederick became so interested in her reading that one day he went to her and asked her to teach him to read. She paused for a while as if in doubt, then she braced up and gave him a lesson. At the end of the lesson his little heart seemed so full of joy and thanks that he scarcely knew what to say or do.

Mrs. Auld, seeing the situation, said, "Run along now, Frederick. I know you are grateful. Come in at this time every day for your lesson." He made his way out and every day for several days, with beaming face, he went in for his lesson.

One day when Mr. Auld came in and saw his wife teaching the boy, he said to her in great surprise, "My dear, are you really teaching that boy to read? Don't you know he will learn to write? Then he will write a pass and run away with himself." She pleaded for Frederick, but Mr. Auld beat upon the door-facing, saying as he went out, "I will have no more of this nonsense. This must be the end of it." Mrs. Auld dismissed Frederick and seemingly repented of her mistake; but Frederick had learned his alphabet.

Soon he managed to get a Webster's spelling-book, which he always carried with him when sent on errands. After this, every time he went out, he made new friends until the very boys who at first pounced upon him at every corner, now began to help him with his spelling lessons. One day while he was on his way to the shipyard, and just after he had gotten a spelling lesson at the corner, it occurred to him that the boys might also help him to learn to write.

While he was in the shipyard, he watched the carpenters finish pieces of timber for the different sides of the ships and mark each piece. For instance, a piece for the larboard side was marked *L* and a piece for the starboard side was marked *S*. He soon learned for what these letters stood and how to make them. When he went out on the next errand, he said to the boys, "You can't make as good an *S* as I can make." Such a challenge had to be met. They all dropped down on their knees and began the contest by making letters on the pavement. Frederick watched closely and learned to make for the first time many other letters. He kept at it until he learned to make them all.

Then, thinking that he should practice on these letters and learn to make them well, he picked out a flour barrel, without letting anyone know what he was doing, and carried it one night into the kitchen loft where he slept. He turned it upside down and propped himself up to it and used it as his desk.

Knowing where little Tommy Auld's old copy-books were, he got one out the next day and took it to the loft. That night while the Aulds were asleep he sat in the loft and wrote between the used lines of the old copy-book.

His desire to learn led him into strange paths. One day as he trotted along on his usual errand, with the rain pelting him in the face and over the head, he thought he spied something in the gutter. He stopped suddenly and peeped further into that filthy gutter. There lay some scattered pages of the Bible. He picked them out of the rubbish, took them home and washed and dried them to read.

For days after that, when he went out, he kept his eyes on the gutters for something else to read. Finding nothing there, he bought a box of shoe polish and a brush which he always took along on his errands. Whenever he passed any one with rusty boots or shoes on he said, "Shine, Mister, shine?" By shining boots and saving up carefully, his pennies grew and grew until he had fifty cents. With this he bought a book called the "Columbian Orator", which he read over and over again.

At the end of Frederick's seventh year in Baltimore, news came that he would be taken back to the plantation on the Eastern Shore on account of the death of his old master. This news came as a shock especially to him, Mrs. Auld and Thomas. The three of them, fearing that he might never return, wept bitterly. He was away only one month before he was sent back to Baltimore. Another change, however, soon took place which called him back again to the Eastern Shore, where he remained for two years.

He was now about sixteen years old, and had to work very hard every day and suffer such punishment that he was tired when night came. Yet he wished so much that his fellow slaves might learn to read that he interested a small class of them, which he taught three nights in every week.

He also organized a Sunday-school class of about thirty young men. This he taught under an old oak tree in the woods until three class leaders in old master's church rushed in upon them one Sabbath and forbade their meeting. Later on, however, the class was again secretly begun with more than forty pupils, many of whom learned to read.

Frederick had been reading the "Columbian Orator" which described the cruelties and injustices of slavery. He had also been thinking of how to obtain his freedom; but the pleasant times with his Sunday-school class had delayed his taking any action in the matter. He had not given up the idea, however, for at the beginning of the year 1836 he made a vow that the year should not end without his trying to gain his freedom. He kept the vow in mind and finally told his secret to several of his companions, who agreed to share in a plan to escape.

They met often by night and every Sunday until the day set for their escape was at hand. They were hoping that no one would betray them, but just at the last minute the news leaked out. The boys were seized, dragged to town and thrown in prison, where they remained for some time.

For three years after Frederick's release from prison he worked in the fields suffering untold hardships. The following three years he worked in a shipyard in Baltimore learning the calker's trade. During these last three years his mind was constantly running back to 1817, the year of his birth. Realizing how the years were passing, he was always thinking of some plan of escape. At last he hit upon what seemed to be a real one.

With arrangements all made for his escape, he arose early one September morning in 1838, put on a sailor's suit which a friend had lent him and started down to the depot just in time to take the train. He also carried what was called a sailor's protection, which had on it the American eagle. A hackman, whom he knew well, arrived at the depot with his baggage just as the train was about to pull out. Frederick grabbed his baggage, hopped on the train just like a sailor and took a seat. The train moved on slowly until it reached a certain river which had to be crossed by a ferry boat. On this boat there was a workman who insisted on knowing Frederick. He asked Frederick where he was going and when he was coming back. He persisted in asking questions until Frederick stole away to another part of the boat. After a short while he reached Wilmington, Delaware, where he took a steamboat to Philadelphia, and the train from there to New York City.

The wonderful sights of this great city seemed to make him forget almost everything except the fact that he was now a fugitive slave. A few hours after reaching New York, to his surprise he met on the street a man whom he had known in Baltimore. This man, also a fugitive, began at once to tell Frederick that there were men in New York City hired to betray fugitives and that he must therefore trust no man with his secret.

This news so disturbed Frederick, that instead of seeking a home, he spent the night among barrels on one of the New York wharves. Unable to remain longer without food or shelter, the next day he sought out on the streets a sailor who befriended him and then took him to the home of a Mr. Ruggles an— "underground railroad station"—where he was hidden for several days. During these days his sweetheart came on from Baltimore and they were married. On the day of their marriage they set out for New Bedford, Massachusetts, where Frederick as a ship's calker might possibly find work. Their money gave out on the way but a "Friend", seeing the situation, paid their fares for the remainder of the journey.

After reaching New Bedford, a room was soon secured in the home of a very good man who liked Frederick's face. They talked of many things, among which was the wisdom of Frederick's changing his name. The man said, "I have just been reading Scott's *Lady of the Lake* and I suggest that you take the name Douglass, for that grand man, Douglass of Scotland."

"Douglass of Scotland? Who was he?" asked Frederick. The good man began by telling the story of the bravery in battle of Douglass of Scotland. Before he had finished his story, Frederick was eager to take the name of Douglass.

He had now a fine-sounding name—Frederick Douglass—but he had neither money nor a job. He started out seeking work at his trade but was told again and again that the calkers there would not work with him. Finally, he was forced to take whatever his hands could find to do. He sawed wood; he shoveled coal. He dug cellars; he removed rubbish from back yards. He loaded and unloaded ships and scrubbed their cabins until he secured steady work.

While he was at his work one day a young man brought him a newspaper edited by a man whose name was William Lloyd Garrison, of whom Douglass had never heard before. This paper, for which he immediately subscribed, was known as "The Liberator". He read every word in the issue which the agent gave him and waited impatiently for the next one to come. When it came, there was in it an article about a grand convention to be held in Nantucket. Douglass read the article to the home people. He said that he needed a vacation, which might well be taken at the time of this convention. The following issue of the paper told still more of the plans for the convention. He concluded that he must attend it.

He went to the convention without any thought of being known to anyone or of taking any part whatever in the meetings. A prominent abolitionist, however, who had heard Frederick speak to his people in a little schoolhouse in New Bedford, sought him out and asked him to say a few words to the convention. When he rose to speak, he was trembling in every limb. He could hardly stand erect.

It seemed to him that he could scarcely say two words without hesitating or stammering, but he went on. As he told of his experiences as a slave, the audience was exceedingly quiet. When he had finished, the people broke into applause and excitement. William Lloyd Garrison, now known as a leading abolitionist, was the next speaker. He spoke with feeling, taking Frederick Douglass as his subject. The audience sat motionless and some people present even wept.

At the close of the meeting, another abolitionist came to Douglass and urged him to become a traveling agent for the Massachusetts Anti-Slavery Society. For two reasons, he did not wish to take such a position. In the first place, having been out of slavery just three years, he was afraid he could not speak well enough to travel in that way; and, secondly, he feared that his former master might hear of him and send for him. The abolitionist, however, unwilling to accept excuses, urged Douglass until finally he consented to travel for three months. Before many days had passed he was on the road as a lecturer against slavery.

One morning he went to Grafton, Massachusetts, and tried to get a place to hold a meeting. But he could not get a hall or even a church. Nevertheless, he was so determined to speak to the people that he went to a hotel and borrowed a dinner bell. Soon he was seen running through the streets like a madman, ringing the bell and crying out, "Frederick Douglass, recently a slave, will speak on Grafton Commons at seven o'clock tonight".

Many came out to hear what such a strange man could say and all left at the close of that open-air meeting apparently more thoughtful than when they came. The next day ministers of the large churches in that town came to him and offered to open their doors for his meetings.

For several years he did nothing but travel and hold meetings. He attended one hundred anti-slavery conventions and spoke at every one of them. During the first three or four months of his travel he told the story of his experiences as a slave. Then he became tired of repeating the same old story and began to show by the manner in which he expressed himself that he was thinking deeply about the whole question of slavery.

"Let us have the facts. Be yourself and tell your story," said his hearers again and again, but Douglass said that he was tired of telling his personal story. He attempted to speak against the injustices heaped upon him and others, but his audiences murmured, saying, "He does not talk like a slave. He does not look or act like one; and, besides he does not tell us where he came from or how he got away; and he is educated, too."

Determined to remove doubt from their minds, Douglass wrote a narrative of his life as a slave and had it published. Now that the story of his life was published, friends like Wendell Phillips, fearing he might be captured and taken back into slavery, advised that he go to Europe. He went and he spoke in all the large cities of England, Scotland and Ireland. In order that he might return home a free man, two women in England, "Friends" they were, started the plan of raising the money with which his freedom was purchased from his old master in Baltimore.

On his return to America, he went to Rochester, New York, and for sixteen years edited there a paper called *The North Star*. So much money was needed for publishing this paper that he even mortgaged his home. For twenty-five years he lived in Rochester. During those years he wrote and lectured and conducted an "underground railroad station" in that city.

Because of the disturbed conditions in his own country at this time, he went to Europe again but returned in six months on account of death in his family. Some of the disturbances which he left behind when he went away had subsided but others had risen. A President of the United States had to be elected. For a long time it seemed that no man was the choice of a majority of the people. Finally, Abraham Lincoln, who had once been a rail-splitter, was elected. Douglass worked hard to help elect Lincoln. He also took part in the terrible Civil War, which had come as a result of the country's disturbances.

As soon as the Governor of Massachusetts issued the order for the many soldiers needed, Douglass enlisted his own sons, Charles and Lewis, from New York State, and took a leading part in raising the Fifty-fourth and Fifty-fifth Massachusetts Negro

Regiments. The first of these soon won fame and a name throughout the country because of its brave attack on Fort Wagner in the hour of trial. In that terrible battle at nightfall, the Fifty-fourth was fearfully cut to pieces, losing nearly half of its officers, among whom was its beloved commander, Colonel Shaw. Douglass, with his son Charles as a recruiting officer, worked steadily until the emancipation of the slaves and the close of the war were brought about.

He greatly rejoiced over the outcome of the war, yet a feeling of sadness seemed to come over him. What was he to do? He felt that he had reached the end of the noblest and best part of his life. He thought of settling on a farm which he might buy with the few thousand dollars which he had saved from the sale of his book, called "My Bondage and Freedom", and from the proceeds of his lectures at home and abroad. The question, however, was soon decided for him. To his surprise, invitations began to pour in upon him from colleges, clubs and literary societies offering him one hundred and even two hundred dollars for a single lecture.

One of the literary societies of Western Reserve College invited him to address its members on one Commencement Day. He had never been inside of a schoolhouse for the purpose of studying, therefore the thought of speaking before college professors and students gave him anxiety. He spent days in study for the occasion. Not being able to find in our libraries a certain book which he needed, he sent to England for it. Not long after his address on that Commencement Day, the thought came to Douglass that the Negro was still in need of the opportunity to vote, and thereby become a citizen. He talked about the question and finally set himself to the task of gaining this right for his people.

His first marked step in the matter was to gain for himself and ten other men an interview with the President of the United States. The discussion on that occasion brought the question practically before the whole American public. The next great step in gaining the ballot for the freedmen was taken in Philadelphia in 1866, at a great convention called the "National Loyalists' Convention", which was attended by the ablest men from all sections of the country.

Douglass's own city, Rochester, New York, elected him to represent her. While he was marching in the long procession through the streets of Philadelphia, he saw standing on the corner of Ninth and Chestnut Streets, the daughter of Miss Lucretia

Auld, under whose window he had sung as a hungry slave boy. He went to her and expressed his surprise and joy at seeing her.

"But what brought you to Philadelphia at this time?" Douglass asked.

She replied, "I heard you were to be here and I came to see you walk in the procession." She followed the procession for several blocks and joined in the applause given Frederick Douglass as he passed.

In that convention, resolutions were finally passed in favor of giving the freedmen the right to vote. Douglass was called forward to speak. The vote passed by that convention, it is said, had its influence in bringing about the passage of the Fifteenth Amendment to the Constitution of the United States.

After the convention, Douglass went to Washington, D. C., as editor of a newspaper. It was not long before he became what is called Elector-at-Large for the State of New York. As such a representative, the Republican party of that state sent him to Washington to carry its sealed vote which went toward electing Grant as President. Douglass later received an invitation to speak at the monument of the unknown loyal dead, at Arlington, on Decoration Day.

Five years later, when he spoke at the unveiling of the Lincoln Monument in Lincoln Park, Washington, D. C., the President of the United States and his Cabinet, judges of the Supreme Court, members of the Senate and the House of Representatives, and many thousands of other citizens were there to listen to him, to honor the memory of Lincoln and to show their appreciation of such a gift from the freedmen.

Douglass was appointed United States Marshal of the District of Columbia. As Marshal he visited the criminal courts every day to see that the criminals received justice. There were also high social duties attached to this office. President Garfield later appointed him Recorder of Deeds of the District of Columbia, at which post he remained for nearly five years. In this position, he was responsible for having recorded in the public records every transfer of property, every deed of trust and every mortgage made in the capital of the nation.

In 1886, two years after he was Recorder of Deeds, he and his wife—the second Mrs. Douglass—made a tour through England, Scotland and Ireland, where they met many great people besides the children of many of Douglass's old friends. His next and last appointment as a high public official was to the office of Minister to Hayti. President Harrison appointed him to this office. The President of Hayti also appointed him to act as commissioner for that country at the Chicago World's Fair in 1893.

Many boys and girls who have read his books admit that they have been inspired by the life he lived in traveling from the log cabin on the Eastern Shore of Maryland to the high and important offices which he held in Washington. The best one of these books is called "My Life and Times, by Frederick Douglass". After his death on February 20, 1895, at his home in Anacostia, District of Columbia, the citizens of Rochester, New York, erected a public monument to his memory.

His epitaph has been written in his own words: *"Do not judge me by the heights to which I may have risen but by the depths from which I have come".*

How I Escaped

Frederick Douglass

Although slavery was a delicate subject, and very cautiously talked about among grown-up people in Maryland, I frequently talked about it, and that very freely, with the white boys. I would sometimes say to them, while seated on a curbstone or a cellar door, "I wish I could be free, as you will be when you get to be men. You will be free, you know, as soon as you are twenty-one, and can go where you like, but I am a slave for life. Have I not as good a right to be free as you have?"

Words like these, I observed, always troubled them; and I had no small satisfaction in drawing out from them, as I occasionally did, that fresh and bitter condemnation of slavery which ever springs from natures unseared and unperverted. Of all consciences, let me have those to deal with, which have not been seared and bewildered with the cares and perplexities of life.

I do not remember ever to have met with a boy while I was in slavery, who defended the system, but I do remember many times, when I was consoled by them, and by them encouraged to hope that something would yet occur by which I would be made free. Over and over again, they have told me that "they believed I had as good a right to be free as they had," and that "they did not believe God ever made anyone to be a slave."

On Monday, the third day of September, 1838, in accordance with my resolution, I bade farewell to the city of Baltimore, and to slavery.

My success was due to address rather than courage; to good luck rather than bravery. My means of escape were provided for me by the very men who were making laws to hold and bind me more securely in slavery. It was the custom in the State of Maryland to require of the free colored people to have what were called free papers. This instrument they were required to renew very often, and by charging a fee for this writing, considerable sums from time to time were collected by the State. In these papers the name, age, color, height, and form of the free man were described, together with any scars or other marks upon his person.

Now more than one man could be found to answer the same general description. Hence many slaves could escape by impersonating the owner of one set of papers; and this was often done as follows: A slave nearly or sufficiently answering the description set forth in the papers, would borrow or hire them till he could by their means escape to a free state, and then, by mail or otherwise, return them to the owner. The operation was a hazardous one for the lender as well as the borrower.

A failure on the part of the fugitive to send back the papers would imperil his benefactor, and the discovery of the papers in possession of the wrong man would imperil both the fugitive and his friend. It was therefore an act of supreme trust on the part of a freeman of color thus to put in jeopardy his own liberty that another might be free. It was, however, not infrequently bravely done, and was seldom discovered. I was not so fortunate as to sufficiently resemble any of my free acquaintances to answer the description of their papers.

But I had one friend—a sailor—who owned a sailor's protection, which answered somewhat the purpose of free papers—describing his person, and certifying to the fact that he was a free American sailor. The instrument had at its head the American eagle, which gave it the appearance at once of an authorized document. This protection did not, when in my hands, describe its bearer very accurately. Indeed, it called for a man much darker than myself, and close examination of it would have caused my arrest at the start.

In order to avoid this fatal scrutiny I had arranged with a hackman to bring my baggage to the train just on the moment of starting, and jumped upon the car myself when the train was already in motion. Had I gone into the station and offered to purchase a ticket, I should have been instantly and carefully examined, and undoubtedly arrested.

In choosing this plan upon which to act, I considered the jostle of the train, and the natural haste of the conductor, in a train crowded with passengers, and relied upon my skill and address in playing the sailor as described in my protection, to do the rest. One element in my favor was the kind feeling which prevailed in Baltimore, and other seaports at the time, towards "those who go down to the sea in ships." "Free trade and sailors' rights" expressed the sentiment of the country just then.

In my clothing I was rigged out in sailor style. I had on a red shirt and a tarpaulin hat and black cravat, tied in sailor fashion, carelessly and loosely about my neck. My knowledge of ships and sailor's talk came much to my assistance, for I knew a ship from stem to stern, and from keelson to cross-trees, and could talk sailor like an "old salt."

On sped the train, and I was well on the way to Havre de Grace before the conductor came into the Negro car to collect tickets and examine the papers of his black passengers. This was a critical moment in the drama. My whole future depended upon the decision of this conductor. Agitated I was while this ceremony was proceeding, but still externally, at least, I was apparently calm and self-possessed. He went on with his duty—examining several colored passengers before reaching me. He was somewhat harsh in tone, and peremptory in manner until he reached me, when, strangely enough, and to my surprise and relief, his whole manner changed.

Seeing that I did not readily produce my free papers, as the other colored persons in the car had done, he said to me in a friendly contrast with that observed towards the others: "I suppose you have your free papers?" To which I answered: "No, sir; I never carry my free papers to sea with me." "But you have something to show that you are a free man, have you not?" "Yes, sir," I answered; "I have a paper with the American eagle on it, that will carry me around the world." With this I drew from my deep sailor's pocket my seaman's protection, as before described. The merest glance at the paper satisfied him, and he took my fare and went on about his business.

This moment of time was one of the most anxious I ever experienced. Had the conductor looked closely at the paper, he could not have failed to discover that it called for a very different looking person from myself, and in that case it would have been his duty to arrest me on the instant, and send me back to Baltimore from the first station.

When he left me with the assurance that I was all right, though much relieved, I realized that I was still in great danger: I was still in Maryland, and subject to arrest at any moment. I saw on the train several persons who would have known me in any other clothes, and I feared they might recognize me, even in my sailor "rig," and report me to the conductor, who would then subject me to a closer examination, which I knew well would be fatal to me.

Though I was not a murderer fleeing from justice, I felt, perhaps, quite miserable as such a criminal. The train was moving at a very high rate of speed for that time of railroad travel, but to my anxious mind, it was moving far too slowly. Minutes were hours, and hours were days during this part of my flight. After Maryland I was to pass through Delaware—another slave State. The border lines between slavery and freedom were the dangerous ones, for the fugitives. The heart of no fox or deer, with hungry hounds on his trail, in full chase, could have beaten more anxiously or noisily than did mine, from the time I left Baltimore till I reached Philadelphia.

The passage of the Susquehanna river at Havre de Grace was made by ferry-boat at that time, on board of which I met a young colored man by the name of Nichols, who came very near betraying me. He was a "hand" on the boat, but instead of minding his business, he insisted upon knowing me, and asking me dangerous questions as to where I was going, and when I was coming back, etc. I got away from my old and inconvenient acquaintance as soon as I could decently do so, and went to another part of the boat.

Once across the river I encountered a new danger. Only a few days before I had been at work on a revenue cutter, in Mr. Price's ship-yard, under the care of Captain McGowan. On the meeting at this point of the two trains, the one going south stopped on the track just opposite to the one going north, and it so happened that this Captain McGowan sat at a window where he could see me very distinctly, and would certainly have recognized me had he looked at me but for a second. Fortunately, in the hurry of the moment, he did not see me; and the trains soon passed each other on their respective ways.

But this was not the only hair-breadth escape. A German blacksmith, whom I knew well, was on the train with me, and looked at me very intently, as if he thought he had seen me somewhere before in his travels. I really believe he knew me, but had no heart to betray me. At any rate he saw me escaping and held his peace.

The last point of imminent danger, and the one I dreaded most, was Wilmington. Here we left the train and took the steamboat for Philadelphia. In making the change here I again apprehended arrest, but no one disturbed me, and I was soon on the broad and beautiful Delaware, speeding away to the Quaker City. On reaching Philadelphia in the afternoon I inquired of a colored man how I could get on to New York? He directed me to the Willow street depot, and thither I went, taking the train that night. I reached New York Tuesday morning, having completed the journey in less than twenty-four hours. Such is briefly the manner of my escape from slavery—and the end of my experience as a slave.

Paul Laurence Dunbar

The Poet
1872-1906

An elevator boy—Paul Laurence Dunbar—a black high-school graduate—stood for a few moments at the entrance to his elevator. He seemed to fix his eyes on every one entering the Callahan Building.

The Callahan Building was a large structure located in a busy section of Dayton, Ohio. Its quick elevator service in spite of its limited number of elevators was often a subject of comment. The grating of the elevator cables and the thud of the car as it stopped for passengers were constant reminders of the rapid service. Up and down, up and down, went the elevator, and ring, ring, went the bells from morning until night. As the elevator moved upward and downward with grating cables, Paul kept his ear turned as though he were listening to a song.

Apparently unnoticed, day after day he ran his elevator, stopping repeatedly first at one floor and then another until one day a woman entered his car and spoke to him. It was one of his former high-school teachers. After greeting him, she eagerly told him that the Western Association of Writers would soon meet in Dayton. Before the short conversation was finished, she asked him to write a poem of welcome to that association and promised that she would arrange for him to recite it.

Paul's busy days seemed to come and go very rapidly. Yet when the Western Association of Writers met a few weeks later he had composed his poem of welcome for the occasion. The printed programs of the association did not contain his name. The first day of the meeting, however, after being excused from his elevator duties, clad as he was, he hurried to the hall in which the sessions were to be held. His teacher stood in the doorway waiting for him. He entered silently and made his way to the rostrum and began reciting his poem of welcome. Men and women in the audience at first straightened up to look at this swarthy lad. Then, as if suddenly struck by something in the poem, many a one turned his ear and leaned forward to listen. When Paul had finished, the entire audience broke into applause. Some even rushed forward to shake his hand.

At the close of the meeting some of the writers looked for the boy poet but he had hurried back to his elevator. Just at the moment when they were about to give up their search for him they ran across his former high-school teacher. She, with enthusiasm exceeding theirs, told of Dunbar's graduating from high-school in 1891 with honors. She told of his composing the class-song which was sung at the commencement exercises. One of the writers interrupted to ask who the boy was and what he was doing. The teacher, speaking hurriedly as though she had something else important to tell first, said that Dunbar was once editor of their high-school paper. She also told of his writing his first poem before he was seven years old. Then proceeding to answer the writer's questions she said that Dunbar's mother was a washerwoman and that he was the elevator boy at the Callahan Building; and looking each of these writers in the face, she added:

"Dunbar always brings and carries the clothes for his mother."

Three of the men, after inquiring where the Callahan Building was, started in search of it. They found it and soon entered the elevator. Among the first things they saw were a *Century* Magazine, a lexicon, a scratch tablet and a pencil lying on a stool. Dunbar was in the act of starting his car when one of the men said: "No! No! Do not go up for us! We came simply to see you and to tell you how much we appreciated the poem you read this morning."

Dunbar looked at them with great embarrassment. As he began to thank them a ring of the elevator signal came from the top floor. With a modest bow and a request to be excused, he took hold of the power lever and up the elevator went and soon down it came again.

In the midst of the conversation, constantly interrupted by passengers entering the elevator, one of the visitors asked, "What wages are you getting here?"

"Four dollars a week, Sir", answered Dunbar.

"What are you doing with your money?" asked another.

Dunbar, somewhat hesitatingly said, "Well, I help my mother and then I am trying to buy a little home for her, too."

"How on earth—?"

Ring, ring, went bells on different floors. Up went the elevator and then down it came.

Hurrying to finish his sentence, the visitor continued, "How on earth did you start to buy a home on four dollars a week? Where is your father?"

Dunbar, disturbed by so many questions and so many bells, said hurriedly, "I bought the home through the Building and Loan Association. My father was a plasterer but he died when I was twelve years old." As another bell began to ring, the men said goodbye and went away talking about the boy and pledging each other to propose his name for membership in the Western Association of Writers.

Dunbar seemed greatly encouraged by the Western Association members. He had also received promises of help from others. One evening, after a hard day on the elevator, he hurried home, saying to his mother as he entered, "Ma, where are those papers I asked you to save for me some months ago?"

"What, those botany sheets?" she replied. Dunbar failed to answer immediately. She continued, "They are in that box under the kitchen safe." The neighbors had begun to ask Mrs. Dunbar why she was keeping all of those papers piled on the table for so long. Seeing ·that so many were noticing the unsightly stacks of papers, she had removed them one day from the crowded little room to the kitchen.

With a lighted lamp in his hand, Dunbar went to the kitchen and pulled out the box. There lay his papers, some of which he had not seen for five or six years. He pulled a chair up to the box and began sorting them. When he had finished and given the box a shove which sent it back under the safe, he made known his readiness for his supper.

The next morning as he was leaving for his work he said, "Goodbye, Ma, I'm going to see about publishing a book today." He walked rapidly to the Callahan Building and immediately took charge of his elevator. As soon as his lunch hour came he hurried to a publishing house and asked to see the manager. He was out to lunch but one of his assistants was called in. After looking the manuscript through hastily he offered to publish it for one hundred and twenty-five dollars. Dunbar looked at him and shook his head. Unable to conceal his disappointment, he took up his manuscript, bade him good-day and started out.

The business manager of the firm happened to come in at this moment and saw Dunbar starting out. He noticed the gloom and the disappointment written on the boy's face, called him over to his desk and asked what was the trouble. Dunbar at first, choking with something which seemed to cut off his words, simply handed him the manuscript, repeating as best he could what the assistant had said about publishing it for one hundred and twenty-five dollars. The business manager took the manuscript and read here and there a poem. He questioned the lad at length about his work and his home. Knowing something about Dunbar's high-school record, he said, "You go back to your work; the poems will be published."

He went on with his work, scarcely waiting for the boy to thank him. Dunbar bowed, stepped away lightly and with a broad smile on his face hurried back to his elevator.

The hours seemed to drag and yet he worked away until closing time came. On leaving his elevator he went by leaps and bounds until he reached his mother's door. With his key in hand, he unlocked it and rushed in almost breathless, saying, "Oh, Ma, they are going to print my book!" As he told the story about the business manager he laughed and cried. Mrs. Dunbar laughed and cried too until far into the night.

As the days came and went, Mrs. Dunbar began to listen with unusual interest for the ringing of the door-bell. Finally, one morning as the snow fell thick and fast, there was a knock at the door. Mrs. Dunbar grabbed up her apron, wiped the soapsuds from her hands and hurried to open it. There stood a delivery man with a large package.

"For Mr. Paul Dunbar," said he. "By the way, who is this Dunbar? Is he a doctor, a lawyer, a preacher, or what?"

Mrs. Dunbar responded, saying, "Who? Paul? Why, Paul is just an elevator boy and a—a poet." The man looked at her with squinting eyes, glanced about at the front of the poor little cottage, then bade her good-day and went his way.

She made a small opening at one end of the package and peeped at the books. Before realizing what she was doing, she threw her arms around the package and knelt down with her head resting on it, offering a silent prayer. When finally she returned to her washtub, she rubbed a garment a while, then wiped away the tears which were dropping into the soapsuds. The wash seemed to hold her unusually long and yet, when she had finished it, the sun was still high in the heavens. She prepared her dinner, did her chores, then sat down to watch and wait. Finally there came a familiar step. She listened for a moment, then rose and opened the door while Dunbar was feeling for his keys.

"See the books, Paul!" she said, pointing to the package. They opened up the package and stood half bent over it while Paul was reading from the little book of poems which he had named "Oak and Ivy". They took it to the dinner table, looked at it, read more from it and rejoiced together.

The next morning, as Dunbar went back to his elevator, he took along some copies of "Oak and Ivy". These he ventured to show to the passengers who he thought might buy a copy. His supply was soon sold out. Greatly surprised at his first day's success, he took more copies the next day, and still more the following days for over a week. In less than two weeks' time, he walked into the office of the business manager of the publishing house, reached into his pocket and pulled out one hundred and twenty-five dollars. This he placed in the business manager's hands, adding his hearty, humble thanks. He told of his success in selling the books on the elevator and left the publishing-house to see a man who was offering him a minor position in the court-house. After serving notice on the employment manager of the Callahan Building and assisting him in securing another elevator boy, Dunbar left to take up his new duties.

Within the next few days he smiled and rejoiced as he read a review of his poems in a newspaper called *The Toledo Blade*. A few days later he began to receive letters from people who had read this review. Still later, some of these people arranged for him to give readings of his poems.

Among those who wrote him about the review was a Dayton woman who sent a copy of "Oak and Ivy" to a Dr. Tobey of Toledo. Dr. Tobey read a few of the poems and laid the book aside. A few weeks later when he went to Dayton on some business, he discovered to his surprise that even the business men were talking about Dunbar and his poems. On his return home, he took up the book and sat down to read the poems again. He sat there reading and re-reading, occasionally stopping between poems as if he were thinking deeply. When he had finished the book he drew his check book from his pocket, made out a check to Dunbar and enclosed it in a letter asking for a number of copies of "Oak and Ivy".

When Dunbar's letter in reply, expressing his deep appreciation for the check, was received, Dr. Tobey seemed to be deeply moved. He wrote Dunbar immediately inviting him to Toledo to give a reading of his poems. The young poet read the letter to his mother and soon began to prepare for the trip. Night after night, until time to go, he practiced reading some of his poems which had not been published. Even while the train sped along to Toledo, he sat saying over and over to himself the words of some of the poems.

After the reading that night, Dr. Tobey and a Mr. Thatcher, who had also helped Dunbar, shook his hand warmly and asked about the new poems. Upon learning that the young poet had a second book ready they at once agreed to furnish the money to publish it. Consequently, a second book of poems called "Majors and Minors" was soon published.

The day that Dr. Tobey received a copy of "Majors and Minors" he was called into a consultation which kept him at a hotel that night. He and a friend sat up reading this little book of poems until midnight. Just as they had finished and stepped up to the desk to get their keys, another man walked up too. He was a great actor playing Monte Cristo at that time in Toledo. Dr. Tobey upon being introduced to him said, "I know you actor folks are always being bored by people wanting you to read and give opinions of poems, but I have something here that I wish you would read if you will."

The actor took the crude little copy of "Majors and Minors" and turned its pages. Dr. Tobey asked him to read a poem entitled "When Sleep Comes Down to Soothe the Weary Eyes". He read it at first quietly as he leaned over the counter. Then he read it aloud. With great expression and gesture he read it a third time. He turned to another poem and read that; then to another and another until the clock struck one—two—three. He took out his watch and looked at it.

"Hello!" he said, "Three o'clock in the morning! Dr. Tobey, I thank you for giving me this opportunity. In my opinion no poet has written such verses since the days of Poe."

Dunbar soon gave up his work and went to Toledo to sell his book. One night after a very discouraging day, he walked into Dr. Tobey's office to tell him his troubles. Dr. Tobey said, "Well, my boy, how goes the battle?"

"Oh, doctor", said Dunbar, with tears streaming down his cheeks, "I never can offer to sell another book to any man."

"Paul," replied Dr. Tobey, "why don't you make up a speech?"

"Oh", answered Paul, "I have tried to do that but my tongue cleaves to the roof of my mouth and I cannot say a word."

The doctor said sympathetically, "You're no good as a book-agent. While I was down town this morning I sold three of your books to three of the most prominent men in Toledo."

Dr. Tobey then advised him to send a copy of "Majors and Minors" to the actor and author of another play which was then being presented in Toledo. Dunbar made several attempts to present the book in person but failed in each attempt. Nevertheless, before leaving Toledo, he saw to it that the book reached the actor. After reading it, the actor wrote Dunbar a most encouraging letter. He also sent a copy of the poems to the novelist, William Dean Howells. This well-known writer in turn sent a full-page review of the poems to *Harper's Monthly*. He described the little book as a countrified little volume in appearance which inwardly was full of a new world. Singular it was that the article appeared in *Harper's Monthly* on the 27th of June, 1896, which was

Dunbar's twenty-fourth birthday. After being told of the article by a friend, Dunbar went to a newsstand and purchased a copy of *Harper's Monthly*. As he read the article, he said he knew not whether to laugh or cry, but no doubt he did a little of each. Hundreds of letters from all parts of the world, even from Athens, Greece, began to pour into the office of the publishers. Some were ordering Dunbar's poems, others were asking for his photograph and still others were asking for information about him.

On the Fourth of July, Dunbar and his mother went, at Dr. Tobey's invitation, to Toledo. When they arrived at the meeting place about sixty prominent persons from Toledo and elsewhere sat waiting to greet them. Dr. Tobey, with his arm about Dunbar's shoulder as they walked towards a little ante-room said, "It has all come at once, Paul. Mr. Howells has made you famous. They all want to meet you now. Those who made fun of you because of your color and your poverty are now eager to clasp your hand. This is going to be the testing day of your life. I hope you will bear good fortune and popularity as well and as bravely as you have met your disappointments and your humiliations. If so, that will indeed be a proof of your greatness."

Among the poems which Dunbar recited that day was "Ships that Pass in the Night". The audience seemed especially moved by this poem. The most prominent man in that select group said, "Of all things I ever heard, I never listened to anything so impressive."

That night, after such a triumphant day, Dunbar, sitting alone, wrote these lines:

Mere human strength may stand ill fortune's frown;
   So I prevailed, for human strength was mine;
But from the killing strength of great renown
   Naught may protect me save a strength Divine.

Help me, O Lord, in this my trembling cause.
I scorn men's curses, but I dread applause.

During these days of public attention, the poet visited some of the eastern cities, giving readings of his works to audiences composed of people from all sections. On almost every occasion, the audience responded with loud applause and often with bursts of laughter.

The following year, when the opportunity to go to England as a reader of his poems presented itself, he took advantage of it. While he was in London, the

American Ambassador arranged an entertainment for him at which he read before many of the foremost men and women of London. He was further entertained by prominent clubs and prominent people. Although he was being royally treated, he often ran away from the public gatherings in London to his lodging place to work on his first novel, "The Uncalled".

One day just as he was nearing the end of this novel, he received a letter from a friend in America asking if he would accept a place in the Library of Congress at Washington, D.C. He wrote the friend immediately thanking him for his interest and assuring him that he would be glad to accept the position if offered.

On his return to America a little later, he went at once to Washington, D. C., where he began his work in the Library of Congress. Among the first things he did was to look up a home for his mother. As soon as they were settled in their home, he began to use his evenings and all of his spare time in writing.

For about fifteen months, he sat at his desk nearly every evening until far into the night. One night he wrote a friend, saying, "I am working very hard these days, so if it is only for the idle that the devil runs his employment bureau, I have no need of his services." By such diligence, he soon had published a third book of poems which he called "Lyrics of Lowly Life".

Apparently great joy and a cessation of undue toil took the place of his very busy days for a while. About this time, he married a young woman who also had written some verses. Both she and he appeared to be very happy until he began to be annoyed by a stubborn, hacking cough. The dust from the library books seemed to aggravate it so that he soon resigned his position. Thinking that a change of climate would do him good, he made a tour of the South, giving readings of his poems as he went.

The cough continued to trouble him. Taking the advice of a physician, he began to prepare to go to the Catskill Mountains. However, before he left, another volume of poems appeared which he had named "Lyrics of the Hearthside". The new volume of poems seemed to give him strength. He completed his preparations and set out for the mountains. While there he worked steadily writing poems and stories. Just as steadily did his cough seem to grow worse. After a while, he began to feel that Denver, Colorado, was the place for him. He consulted a physician and was not long in starting out for Denver, accompanied by Mrs. Dunbar and his mother.

The long trip seemed to tire him greatly and yet he reached Denver in safety. After a few days' rest, he did his best at strolling around looking at the mountainous country. One day, as he sat writing a friend, he said, "Well, it is something to sit down under the shadow of the Rocky Mountains even if one only goes there to die."

After securing a little house in a town near Denver, he bought an old mare, which he hitched every morning to his buggy and drove for miles. One day after a long, long ride over the beautiful hills he sat down and wrote a poem about "That Ol' Mare of Mine". Although he could not walk much, he worked for hours each day until he had finished a novel which he called "The Love of Landry".

After spending some months in Denver, he and Mrs. Dunbar returned to Washington, D.C., where they bought a home and apparently settled down. The home, however, was soon closed. He went first to Chicago and then to Dayton, where his mother had returned.

Although his cough was about as bad as it could be, he was working on another volume of poems which came out during the early winter months of 1903 under the title of "Lyrics of Love and Laughter".

During the seven years of his illness, he often received his friends. Sometimes he even served tea for them. Once a friend who had business in Dayton called him by telephone saying that she was coming out to see him. When she reached his home, there he was curled up on a couch for all the world like a small boy. He was writing a poem just to please her. Said he on her arrival, "Just wait a moment, I'm hunting for a rhyme." And sure enough, in just a few moments he handed her a scrap of paper on which was written:

TO A POET AND A LADY

You sing, and the gift of State's applause
　Is yours for the rune that is ringing.
But tell me truly, is that the cause?
　Don't you sing for the love of singing?

You think you are working for wealth and for fame,
　But ah, you are not, and you know it;
For wife is the sweetest and loveliest name,
　And every good wife is a poet!

Dunbar continued to write stories and poems almost to the day of his death, which came on the 9th day of February, 1906. His last poem he never wrote down, but simply dictated to his stenographer.

The Boy and the Bayonet

Paul Laurence Dunbar

It was June, and nearing the closing time of school. The air was full of the sound of bustle and preparation for the final exercises, field day, and drills. Drills especially, for nothing so gladdens the heart of the Washington mother, be she black or white, as seeing her boy in the blue cadet's uniform, marching proudly to the huzzas of an admiring crowd. Then she forgets the many nights when he has come in tired out and dusty from his practice drill, and feels only the pride and elation of the result.

Although Tom did all he could outside of study hours, there were many days of hard work for Hannah Davis, when her son went into the High School. But she took it upon herself gladly, since it gave Bud the chance to learn, that she wanted him to have. When, however, he entered the Cadet Corps it seemed to her as if the first steps toward the fulfilment of all her hopes had been made. It was a hard pull to her, getting the uniform, but Bud himself helped manfully, and when his mother saw him rigged out in all his regimentals, she felt that she had not toiled in vain.

And in fact it was worth all the trouble and expense just to see the joy and pride of "little sister," who adored Bud.

As the time for the competitive drill drew near there was an air of suppressed excitement about the little house on "D" Street, where the three lived. All day long "little sister," who was never very well and did not go to school, sat and looked out of the window on the uninteresting prospect of a dusty thoroughfare lined on either side with dull red brick houses, all of the same ugly pattern, interspersed with older, uglier, and viler frame shanties. In the evening Hannah hurried home to get supper against the time when Bud should return, hungry and tired from his drilling, and the chore work which followed hard upon its heels.

Things were all cheerful, however, for as they applied themselves to the supper, the boy, with glowing face, would tell just how his company "A" was getting on, and what they were going to do to companies "B" and "C." It was not boasting so much as the expression of a confidence, founded upon the hard work he was doing, and Hannah and the "little sister" shared that with him.

The child often, listening to her brother, would clap her hands or cry, "Oh, Bud, you're just splendid an' I know you'll beat 'em."

"If hard work'll beat 'em, we've got 'em beat," Bud would reply, and Hannah, to add an admonitory check to her own confidence, would break in with, "Now, don't you be too sho'; dey ain't been no man so good dat dey wasn't somebody bettah." But all the while her face and manner were disputing what her words expressed.

The great day came, and it was a wonderful crowd of people that packed the great baseball grounds to overflowing. It seemed that all of Washington's colored population was out, when there were really only about one-tenth of them there. It was an enthusiastic, banner-waving, shouting, hallooing crowd. Its component parts were strictly and frankly partisan, and so separated themselves into sections differentiated by the colors of the flags they carried and the ribbons they wore. Side yelled defiance at side, and party bantered party. Here the blue and white of company "A" flaunted audaciously on the breeze beside the very seats over which the crimson and gray of "B" were flying and they in their turn nodded defiance over the imaginary barrier between themselves and "C's" black and yellow.

The band was thundering out Sousa's "High School Cadet's March," the school officials, the judges, and reporters, and some with less purpose were bustling about discussing and conferring. Altogether doing nothing much with beautiful unanimity. All was noise, hurry, gaiety, and turbulence.

In the midst of it all, with blue and white rosettes pinned on their breasts, sat two spectators, tense and silent, while the breakers of movement and sound struck and broke around them. It seemed too much to Hannah and "little sister" for them to laugh and shout. Bud was with company "A," and so the whole program was more like a religious ceremonial to them. The blare of the brass to them might have been the trumpet call to battle in old Judea, and the far-thrown tones of the megaphone the voice of a prophet proclaiming from the hill-top.

Hannah's face glowed with expectation, and "little sister" sat very still and held her mother's hand save when amid a burst of cheers company "A" swept into the parade ground at a quick step, then she sprang up, crying shrilly, "There's Bud! there's Bud! I see him!"

and then settled back into her seat overcome with embarrassment. The mother's eyes danced as soon as the sister's had singled out their dear one from the midst of the blue-coated boys, and it was an effort for her to keep from following her little daughter's example even to echoing her words.

Company "A" came swinging down the field toward the judges in a manner that called for more enthusiastic huzzas that carried even the Freshmen of other commands "off their feet." They were, indeed, a set of fine-looking young fellows, brisk, straight, and soldierly in bearing. Their captain was proud of them, and his very step showed it. He was like a skilled operator pressing the key of some great mechanism, and at his command they moved like clockwork. Seen from the side it was as if they were all bound together by inflexible iron bars, and as the end man moved all must move with him.

The crowd was full of exclamations of praise and admiration, but a tense quiet enveloped them as company "A" came from columns of four into line for volley firing. This was a real test; it meant not only grace and precision of movement, singleness of attention and steadiness, but quickness tempered by self-control. At the command the volley rang forth like a single shot. This was again the signal for wild cheering and the blue and white streamers kissed the sunlight with swift impulsive kisses. Hannah and "little sister" drew closer together and pressed hands.

The "A" adherents, however, were considerably cooled when the next volley came out, badly scattering, with one shot entirely apart and before the rest. Bud's mother did not entirely understand the sudden quieting of the adherents; they felt vaguely that all was not as it should be, and the chill of fear laid hold upon their hearts. What if Bud's company (it was always Bud's company to them), what if his company should lose. But, of course, that couldn't be. Bud himself had said that they would win. Suppose, though, they didn't; and with these thoughts they were miserable until the cheering again told them that the company had redeemed itself.

Someone behind Hannah said, "They are doing splendidly, they'll win, they'll win yet in spite of the second volley."

Company "A," in columns of four, had executed the right oblique in double time, and halted amid cheers; then formed left front into line without halting. The next movement was one looked forward to with much anxiety on account of its difficulty. The order was marching by fours to fix or unfix bayonets. They were going at a quick step, but the boys' hands were steady—hope was bright in their hearts. They were doing it rapidly and freely, when suddenly from the ranks there was the bright gleam of steel lower down than it should have been. A gasp broke from the breasts of company "A's" friends. The blue and white dropped disconsolately, while a few heartless ones who wore other colors attempted to hiss. Someone had dropped his bayonet. But with muscles unquivering, without a turned head, the company moved on as if nothing had happened, while one of the judges, an army officer, stepped into the wake of the boys and picked up the fallen steel.

No two eyes had seen half so quickly as Hannah and "little sister's" who the blunderer was. In the whole drill there had been but one figure for them, and that was Bud,—Bud, and it was he who had dropped his bayonet. Anxious, nervous with the desire to please them, perhaps with a shade too much of thought of them looking on with their hearts in their eyes, he had fumbled, and lost all he was striving for. His head went round and round and all seemed black before him.

He executed the movements in a dazed way. The applause, generous and sympathetic, as his company left the parade ground, came to him from afar off, and like a wounded animal he crept away from his comrades, not because their reproaches stung him, for he did not hear them, but because he wanted to think what his mother and "little sister" would say, but his misery was as nothing to that of the two who sat up there amid the ranks of the blue and white, holding each other's hands with a despairing grip. To Bud all of the rest of the contest was a horrid nightmare; he hardly knew when the three companies were marched back to receive the judges' decision. The applause that greeted company "B" when the blue ribbons were pinned on the members' coats meant nothing to his ears. He had disgraced himself and his company. What would his mother and his "little sister" say?

To Hannah and "little sister," as to Bud, all of the remainder of the drill was a misery. The one interest they had had in it failed, and not even the dropping of his gun by one of company "E" when on the march, halting in line, could raise their spirits. The little girl tried to be brave, but when it was all over she was glad to hurry out before the crowd got started and to hasten away home. Once there and her tears flowed freely; she hid her face in her mother's dress, and sobbed as if her heart would break.

"Don't cry, Baby! don't cry, Lammie, dis ain't da las' time da wah goin' to be a drill. Bud'll have a chance anotha time and den he'll show 'em somethin'; bless you, I spec' he'll be a captain." But this consolation of philosophy was nothing to "little sister." It was so terrible to her, this failure of Bud's. She couldn't blame him, she couldn't blame anyone else, and she had not yet learned to lay all such unfathomed catastrophes at the door of fate. What to her was the thought of another day; what did it matter to her whether he was a captain or a private? She didn't even know the meaning of the words, but "little sister," from the time she knew Bud was a private, thought that was much better than being a captain or any other of those things with a long name, so that settled it.

Her mother finally set about getting the supper, while "little sister" drooped disconsolately in her own little splint-bottomed chair. She sat there weeping silently until she heard the sound of Bud's step, then sprang up and ran away to hide. She didn't dare to face him with tears in her eyes. Bud came in without a word and sat down in the dark front room.

"Dat you, Bud?" asked his mother.

"Yassum."

"Bettah come now, supper's puty 'nigh ready."

"I don't want no supper."

"You bettah come on. Bud, I reckon you's mighty tired."

He did not reply, but just then a pair of thin arms were put around his neck and a soft cheek was placed close to his own.

"Come on, Buddie," whispered "little sister," "Mammy an' me know you didn't mean to do it, an' we don't keer."

Bud threw his arms around his little sister and held her tightly.

"It's only you an' ma I care about," he said, "though I am sorry I spoiled the company's drill; they say "B" would have won anyway on account of our bad firing, but I did want you and ma to be proud."

"We is proud," she whispered, "we's mos' prouder dan if you'd won," and pretty soon she led him by the hand to supper.

Hannah did all she could to cheer the boy and to encourage him to hope for next year, but he had little to say in reply, and went to bed early.

In the morning, though it neared school time, Bud lingered around and seemed in no disposition to get ready to go.

"Bettah git ready fer school," said Hannah cheerily.

"I don't believe I want to go anymore," Bud replied.

"Not go anymore? Why, ain't you 'shamed to talk that way! O' cose you goin' to school."

"I'm ashamed to show my face to the boys."

"What you say about de boys? De boys ain't a-goin' to give you an edgication when you need it."

"Oh, I don't want to go, ma; you don't know how I feel."

"I'm kinder sorry I let you go into dat company," said Hannah musingly, " 'cause it was de teachin' I wanted you to git, not the prancin' and steppin'; but I did t'ink it would make mo' of a man of you, an' it ain't. Yo' pappy was a po' man, ha'd wo'kin', an' he wasn't high-toned neither, but from the time I first see him to the day of his death, I nevah seen him back down because he was afeared of anything," and Hannah turned to her work.

"Little sister" went up and slipped her hand in his. "You ain't a-goin to back down, is you, Buddie?" she said.

"No," said Bud stoutly, as he braced his shoulders, "I'm a-goin'."

But no persuasion could make him wear his uniform.

The boys were a little cold to him, and some were brutal. But most of them recognized the fact that what had happened to Tom Harris might have happened to any one of them. Besides, since the percentage had been shown, it was found that "B" had outpointed them in many ways, and so their loss was not due to the one grave error.

Bud's heart sank when he dropped into his seat in the Assembly Hall to find seated on the platform one of the blue-coated officers who had acted as judge the day before. After the opening exercises were over he was called upon to address the school. He spoke readily and pleasantly, laying especial stress upon the value of discipline; toward the end of his address he said "I suppose company 'A' is heaping accusations upon the head of the young man who dropped his bayonet yesterday." Tom could have died. "It was most regrettable," the officer continued, "but to me the most significant thing at the drill was the conduct of that cadet afterward. I saw the whole proceeding; I saw that he did not pause for an instant, that he did not even turn his head, and it appeared to me as one of the finest bits of self-control I had ever seen in any youth; had he forgotten himself for a moment and stopped, however quickly, to secure the weapon, the next line would have been interfered with and your whole movement thrown into confusion." There were a half hundred eyes glancing furtively at Bud, and the light began to dawn in his face. "This boy has shown what discipline means, and I for one want to shake hands with him, if he is here."

When he had concluded the Principal called Bud forward, and the boys, even his detractors, cheered as the officer took his hand.

"Why are you not in uniform, sir?" he asked.

"I was ashamed to wear it after yesterday," was the reply.

"Don't be ashamed to wear your uniform," the officer said to him, and Bud could have fallen on his knees and thanked him.

There were no more jeers from his comrades, and when he related it all at home that evening there were two more happy hearts in that South Washington cottage.

"I told you we was more prouder dan if you'd won," said "little sister."

"An' what did I tell you 'bout backin' out?" asked his mother.

Bud was too happy and too busy to answer; he was brushing his uniform.

Booker Taliaferro Washington

Educator, Orator, Author, Statesman
1859-1915

I
Boyhood and Youth

Early one winter morning, about sixty years ago, a big rooster began flapping his wings and crowing—flap, flap, flap—cock-a-doodle-doo, cock-a-doodle-doo. Then a little rooster began cock-a-doodle-doo, cock-a-doodle-doo. Then here, there and everywhere was the sound—flap, flap, cock-a-doodle-doo—until all Franklin County, Virginia, seemed to have wings and crowing apparatus.

In the midst of this flapping and crowing, young Booker awoke, rubbed his eyes and yawned. Then he jumped out of bed, his feet striking the earthen floor and his teeth chattering in spite of the blazing fire before him. The wind, whistling through the cracks in the sides and the roof of the cabin, evidently made the dirt floor very cold to his feet.

He dressed quickly, having only three pieces to put on—a flax shirt and two wooden shoes. As the coarse shirt began to slip down over his back, it felt so much like pin points or chestnut burrs against his flesh, that he cried "Ouch, Ouch!" as he straightened out the folds of his shirt. Then he sat on the side of the bed to put on his wooden shoes. He pulled at the pieces of rough leather on the tops of them. He twisted and turned his feet until they adjusted themselves as best they could to the shape of the wooden shoes. As he started toward the fire, the sound of his shoes—blump, blump, blump—caused his mother to look around.

She, being the plantation cook, had been so busy getting breakfast for fifty or more plantation hands that she had scarcely noticed Booker until now. "Good morning, son," she said, "run out to the pan and wash your face. Ma wishes you to get out some sweet potatoes."

Booker could not run very fast in his stiff shoes but he went out as quickly as he could, carrying a gourd of water in his hand. He washed his face and soon returned with a field hoe on his shoulder. After removing several boards from the top of the potato hole in the middle of the dirt floor, he began to dig into it with his hoe. First he dug out some of the loose earth and then some of the straw. He dropped down on his knees and pulled out many potatoes with his hands. After clearing a place for them on the hearth, his mother covered them over with hot ashes.

With a long, flat iron she turned the burning coals from the big skillet lids. The smell of the corn-pone and of the roasting potatoes so tantalized the cat that she slid in through the cat hole in the lower right-hand corner of the cabin wall.

Men, women and children hurried from all parts of the plantation to snatch a bite to eat at this little cabin. Many mouths were busy eating corn-bread and molasses. Here and there a crust of bread was used as a knife and fork but many just plunged their fingers into the molasses and bread.

Booker stood like the other children with his tin pan while molasses was being poured into it. He tipped the edges of the pan first this way and then that way so that the molasses might run all over the bottom of it.

Several months later things were all changed. There was no need of a plantation cook, and so Booker's mother was getting ready to go away. One morning as some of those same roosters flapped their wings and crowed for day, a rough little cart rolled up to her cabin door. Booker, his brother John, and his mother hurried around, grabbed up their few bed clothes, stools and skillets and threw them into the cart. "Goodbye, goodbye," they said to their friends. And off they started to join Booker's stepfather in Malden, West Virginia.

For two weeks they traveled, sleeping in the open air and cooking their food out-of-doors over a log fire. One night they started to camp in an old empty log cabin. Just as the fire had gotten well started and their pallet on the floor was made, a large black snake fully a yard and a half long dropped down the chimney and glided across the floor. They ran out of the cabin and later removed their things from it. The next day they continued their journey.

Early one evening, as they began to drive more slowly in search of a good place to stop for the night, a rider came by with his horse in a gallop and bowed to them. Booker called out, "Mister, how far is it to Malden?"

The man did not stop but answered, saying, "About two miles over the hill."

The little cart rolled on until it seemed that they had gone ten miles over the hill instead of two. Finally they heard men swearing and quarreling. They saw men fighting and drinking and gambling. Suddenly a man stepped up and greeted them, "Hello, hello, howdy, howdy." It was Booker's stepfather who had come to Malden several years before.

"Oh, what is that, Pa?" Booker exclaimed, "over there where the light is?"

"That is only a salt furnace," he answered. "There are plenty of them here. I have a job waiting for you in one of them." In a few days, just as he had been told, Booker was at his new job in a salt furnace.

In this part of the town, in that part and all about, people were asking each other, "Have you heard of the school that is to open in Malden? They tell me that the teacher is already here and that old folks as well as children can go to it."

This question was asked young Booker. His eyes sparkled and his face lighted up on hearing such good news. Then he said in an undertone, "Oh, well, I can't go to school anyway for I have to work all day."

When the school began there were many happy faces, old and young. Every night Booker inquired about the school and tried to show his mother and stepfather how he could work and go to school too.

After a great deal of talking about it, they arranged one night for Booker to go to work at four o'clock in the morning, work until nine o'clock, then go to school and return to his work after school.

The next morning, at nine o'clock, Booker started off to school on a trot. When he reached the school-room door, panting for breath, all eyes were turned upon him, especially because he did not have on a hat. He hesitated a moment but went in just the same and took a seat.

The teacher was calling the roll. "John Jones," he called. "Present," said John Jones. "Mary Ann Roberts," he added. "Present," said Mary Ann Roberts. And on he went until he came to the end of the roll.

Then he turned to Booker and asked his name. Booker twisted and turned for a few moments and said nothing, because he knew he had no name except Booker. Suddenly he remembered hearing about a great man whose name was Washington. When the teacher asked his name again, he jumped up from his seat, and with one hand raised, said, "My name is Booker Washington." He had found a name for himself that day. That night his mother sewed two pieces of cloth together and made him a hat.

He seemed very happy at school. One afternoon he and his classmates—about fifteen of them—were sitting on a long pine-log bench, rocking to and fro and singing out their spelling lesson—"b-a, k-e-r, baker; m-a, k-e-r, maker; s-h-a, k-e-r, shaker." There was a knock at the door. Everybody was silent. The door opened and in walked Booker's stepfather. He quietly explained to the teacher that he had gotten Booker a good job in the coal mines and Booker would have to stop school. The next morning Booker entered a coal mine. He hesitated a little at first about working there because of the darkness.

In this mine one day, he overheard two men talking of Hampton Institute. He crept along in the darkness of the mine, close enough to hear what they were saying. One of the men said, "Yes, they tell me that Negro boys and girls can work their way through that school." The conversation continued. Booker Washington eagerly grasped every word; and he made up his mind on the spot to go to Hampton Institute that fall.

That fall, in 1872, with a cheap little satchel of clothes across his shoulder, he started out for Hampton Institute. The journey was long and there were no through trains, therefore stage coaches were used much of the way. Booker sat back in the stage-coach as the horses trotted along, counting his little money and wondering what he would do when it was all spent. Most of his earnings had been used by his stepfather. When there was nothing left in his pockets, he walked some and begged rides on wagons until he reached Richmond, Virginia. It was late in the night and he did not have a penny left.

He walked and begged for a place to sleep until he was tired out. Soon he spied a high, board sidewalk. After looking around and assuring himself that no one saw him, he crept under it and slept for the rest of the night. For some days he worked in Richmond and slept under the board sidewalk at night.

When he had earned enough to pay his railroad fare on to Hampton Institute, he started out again and reached there with just fifty cents in his pocket. He was tired; he was hungry; he was dirty; he was everything but discouraged. One of the northern teachers looked him over and was not sure apparently that he had come to the right place. While he stood anxiously waiting, he saw others freely admitted to the school.

The teacher finally turned to him, saying, "Well, come with me." He followed her to a recitation room.

She said, pointing to the room, "You may sweep that room." He swept the room three times. He moved every piece of furniture and swept. He swept every closet and corner. He dusted everything four times. He dusted the wood-work around the walls. He dusted every table and table leg. He dusted every bench.

Then he returned to the teacher and said, "Well, I am through with that job."

She went to the door of the room, walked in and looked into every corner and closet. She took out her handkerchief and rubbed it over benches and wood-work. Unable to find one bit of dirt anywhere, she said, "I guess you will do to enter this school."

His first two nights at Hampton Institute were somewhat trying ones. Although he was thirteen years old, he had never used a sheet on his bed; and now there were two sheets on his bed. The first night he slept under both of them and the second night he slept on top of both of them. However, with the help of older boys he learned the right way. He paid his expenses that year by working as a janitor. He brought in coal. He made fires. He removed ashes. He swept and dusted class-rooms.

Summer time came and Booker Washington had nothing to do. He scratched his head as he thought of selling his coat or of trying several other plans, none of which, he feared, would work. A hotel job opened up to him. He took it and by working hard that summer and washing his own clothes, he saved all the money which he earned.

Several more summers and winters of hard work came and went. Finally one June morning in 1875, the Hampton teachers were busy decorating the little chapel for the commencement exercises. People began to gather. The students took their places. The choir began to sing. The graduating class marched in and at the head of the line marched a young man who was calling himself now Booker Taliaferro Washington. He had learned that his mother had named him Booker Taliaferro when he was born.

II
Educator: Tuskegee Institute

One evening just six years after Booker Washington's graduation from Hampton Institute, he and General Samuel Chapman Armstrong, the founder and principal of Hampton Institute, were walking to the railroad station. General Armstrong was talking earnestly, shaking his head and making gestures now and then. He was telling Booker Washington why he had asked him instead of any other boy to go to Tuskegee, Alabama. Washington was listening without saying a word. Just as they reached the station, the sound, t-o-o-t, t-o-o-t, rang out up the road. Then, clang, cling, cling, chuff, che-e-e was heard.

The train stopped with a sudden jolt. Booker Washington grasped General Armstrong's hand. They shook like warm friends and bade each other goodbye. The former, with his bag in his hand, stepped upon the platform just as the bell rang and the train began to move. He glanced out of the window at the General, waved his hand and sat down.

Apparently he tried to look out of the window and forget everything but he kept thinking of what General Armstrong had said about his work—of his two years of teaching at Malden, his night school, his debating club with one of his big, brawny boy debaters waving his hand and saying, "Most honorable judges, I have proven to you that the pen is mightier than the sword." He reached into his bag and took out a picture of the little library which he had started for the school. He looked at it a long time, then he brought forth a letter which a friend had written him the year he was studying at Wayland Seminary, Washington, D.C., and read that.

He placed his things back into his bag, stretched himself a little, yawned and fell asleep. Before the break of day he awoke and read several other letters telling of some of his experiences at Hampton Institute: for instance, his teaching the new Indian boys how to brush their teeth, how to comb and brush their hair, how to wash their hands and faces. One of the letters described Booker Washington's work in organizing the Hampton Institute night-school and teaching in it.

Just at that moment, the train gave a sudden jolt which seemed to shake him out of his deep reverie. He straightened up and began to plan what he would do when he reached Tuskegee. He traveled on for nearly two days listening to the porter call out the names of the many towns and cities as the train reached them. At last he heard the call, "Tuskegee, all out for Tuskegee!" He caught up his bag and hustled out.

He looked all around; but seeing no one looking for him he went ahead making inquiries about the building in which he was to open his school. He looked here and there for several days but the only buildings he could find for his use were an old, dilapidated church and an old shanty with an old chicken-house nearby.

After making arrangements for the use of these old buildings and hiring an old mule and a little wagon to take him over the country, he set out and visited the country people for miles around. He ate with them in their little log cabins. He often used the one and only fork on the table and passed it on to somebody else. That person used it and passed it on to the next person. Around that fork went until everybody at the table had had a chance to use it. He often slept with a family in its one-room cabin when there were so many in that family that he had to go out of doors to undress and dress. Still he kept on visiting for several months until he had seen what the people needed, and had advertised his school.

On the morning of July 4, 1881, the doors of the old dilapidated church in Tuskegee were pulled as wide open as the sagging walls would permit. An old cracked bell was rung, and in walked thirty pupils, some of whom were forty years old. Not one was less than fifteen years old. Every one worked hard and things went well until one day a hard rain came. Water streamed in upon Mr. Washington so that a pupil had to hold an umbrella over him while he heard the recitations.

Six weeks of such teaching passed and then another teacher, Miss Olivia Davidson of Ohio, came to assist Mr. Washington. She taught school and gave festivals and suppers in order to raise five hundred dollars to pay for a school farm. All of the people for miles around wanted to help the school. Some brought five cents; some brought stalks of sugar cane. Others brought quilts.

One old lady about seventy years old, clad in just clean rags, hobbled in one morning on a cane. She said, "Mr. Washington, God knows I spent the best days of my life in slavery. God knows I am ignorant and poor; but I know what you and Miss Davidson are trying to do. I know you are trying to make better men and better women of my race. I haven't any money, but I want you to take these six eggs which I've been saving up, and I want you to put these six eggs into the education of these boys and girls."

Mr. Washington and his assistant worked very hard to raise the five hundred dollars and to get the school started well. He knew how much the farm would mean to the school. He knew also that the students did not like clearing the land and working the field, and so one day he planned what he called a "chopping bee". With his ax swung across his shoulder he led the students out to the farm and made a challenge to outchop any of them. The old ones chopped and the young ones chopped. The boys chopped and the girls chopped. All of them chopped but none outchopped their teacher, Booker Washington.

Boys and girls who look at the picture of Tuskegee Institute as it is today will probably say: "My! Can this be the school for which the old lady brought the six eggs? Can this be the school for which the 'chopping bee' was held?"

It is really that same school. Booker Washington and his assistants worked so faithfully and well that Tuskegee Institute has received not only the six eggs but hundreds of thousands of dollars. The gifts had increased so that when Tuskegee Institute was thirty-four years old it owned two thousand four hundred acres of land, with one hundred and eleven buildings on the grounds. In addition to this, Tuskegee Institute had about twenty thousand acres of land given it by the United States Government as an endowment. The number of students in thirty-four years had increased from thirty to about two thousand and the number of teachers had increased from one to two hundred.

In the early days the school had a dark basement dining-room but now there is a large dining-hall on the campus. In the early days the few knives and forks had to be passed around among the students almost continuously during a meal; but now there are sufficient knives and forks for all. Once upon a time the students used rough boxes and stools for dining-room seats but now there are dining-room chairs for all. In the early days Tuskegee Institute had no kitchen. Blazing fires were made out of doors upon which pots and skillets were set for cooking. Many a time a girl would step on a live coal, throw down the skillet lid and hop away to nurse her burn for a moment; now there are modern kitchens at Tuskegee Institute.

Perhaps you have already begun to think that Tuskegee Institute with about one hundred large brick buildings must look like a little city. It really does. All the buildings and the grounds are lighted by the school's own electric plant. Many industries such as domestic science, carpentry and blacksmithing are taught.

The brick-making industry at Tuskegee Institute is an evidence of the fact that Booker Washington believed in the saying, "If at first you don't succeed, try, try again." He and his students of the early days made their first brick kiln for burning bricks, but the kiln would not work. They made a second kiln and that was a failure; a third brick kiln with about 25,000 bricks in it fell in the middle of the night just when the bricks were nearly ready to be taken out. This seemed like hard luck, but it appears that Booker Washington was never in all his life wholly discouraged at anything. He started a fourth brick kiln with the $15 which he secured by pawning his watch. Today 1,200,000 first-class bricks are manufactured in one season by the students of Tuskegee Institute.

Every day in the year visitors go to Tuskegee Institute from all parts of the world. They go to the shops where the boys are busy making wagons, buggies, cabinets and all sorts of things. They go to the trades building where the girls are cooking, sewing, making hats and doing laundry work. They go to the hospital, to the library, to the classrooms, to the dining-hall and other buildings. They go to the farm, to the piggery, to the dairy farm. They go to the chapel. They hear the students sing and see them march out. Now and then at chapel exercises they see a girl or a boy called out of a long line because a button is off, or shoes are not polished, or clothing is not neat and tidy.

These visitors go away saying to their friends that Booker Washington was certainly a great man. Some go to their homes far away and start schools like Tuskegee Institute. Other visitors have been there, studied the school and gone away to do honor to Booker Washington.

III
Orator, Author, Statesman

In 1896 Harvard University, one of the greatest colleges in the country, honored Booker Washington. He spoke at the University and was later given the degree of Master of Arts. Five years later, another great institution, Dartmouth College, invited him there and gave him the degree of Doctor of Laws.

Wherever he spoke, people came from far and near to hear him. He spoke once in Essex Hall in London, England, and once at Bristol, England.

Just after the Spanish-American War, he was the peace-celebration speaker at the Chicago

Auditorium. In the auditorium that day there were thousands of people, among whom was the President of the United States. And many thousands were on the outside trying to hear Booker Washington speak.

In the middle of his speech he said as he walked across the platform, "Nobody should help a lazy, shiftless person." Then he smiled, opened his eyes wide and said, "Let me tell you this story: Once there were two men seeking to cross a river by means of a ferry boat. The fare across was three cents. One of the men, who seemed to be shiftless and lazy, said to the other, 'Please let me have three cents to cross the ferry; I haven't a penny'. The other man said to him, 'I am sorry not to accommodate you, boss, but the fact is that a man who hasn't three cents is just as bad off on one side of the river as he is on the other'". The audience laughed and applauded.

He said further: "But let me tell you, my friends, everybody is not like the man who did not have three cents. Early one morning not long ago, I was out watching my chickens and pigs. A pig I think is one of the grandest of animals. Old Aunt Caroline came striding by with a basket on her head. I said to her, 'Where are you going, Aunt Caroline?' She replied,

'Lord bless you, Mr. Washington, I've already been where I was going.'" The audience laughed again.

The singing that day lifted one up and made one feel like marching and humming. Some of the poor people present wept for joy, and at the close of the meeting Booker Washington shook hands with many of them. He seemed to understand them and to know their needs. When he wrote his book, "Up from Slavery," much of which was written on the train, he told how poor he himself was once.

Dr. Washington traveled all over the North, East, West and South. He traveled in a special car through Arkansas, Oklahoma, Mississippi, Tennessee, South Carolina, North Carolina, Delaware, Texas, Florida, Louisiana, parts of Alabama, Georgia, Virginia and West Virginia.

His friends began to say, "Dr. Washington looks tired. Let us send him and his wife to Europe on a vacation." They gave his school a large sum of money. Then they talked with his wife, Mrs. Margaret Murray Washington, who was a graduate of a great college called Fisk University. She had helped Dr. Washington for some years in his work and knew how tired he must be. These friends talked and urged until she agreed to go too.

All arrangements for the trip were completed. Dr. and Mrs. Washington bade goodbye to their friends, sailed across the ocean, and for three months went here and there through Holland, Belgium, France and England. He crossed the ocean a second time and then a third time. On these trips kings and queens entertained him and honored him. In his own country, presidents of the United States called him in to talk over important matters.

Following one of his trips abroad, he wrote a book called "The Man Farthest Down", in which he told many sad stories about the poor and ignorant of Europe. He wrote about the women whom he saw in Europe hitched with oxen ploughing the fields. Among his other books are: "The Future of the American Negro", "A History of the Negro" and "Working with the Hands".

He worked hard and seemed to hammer out success in everything. No one called him conceited and yet he had great confidence in himself even to the last. When the doctors in New York told him that he had but a few hours to live, he said, "Then I must start now for Tuskegee." He was a very sick man and could hardly walk when he reached the station but he refused to be carried to the train in an invalid's chair.

For many hours the train sped southward before it reached Cheehaw, the junction station for Tuskegee. A smile came over his face as he drew near the school.

However, he did not live many hours after reaching home. It had been his custom to rise early every morning, and so early in the morning on the 14th of November, 1915, Booker T. Washington, the chieftain and the servant of all peoples, rose and departed to the land of the blessed.

For the next few days, the Tuskegee Institute grounds, even as large as they are, were almost packed with people from near and far. The poor, uneducated people, black and white, from the cotton fields of Alabama were there. Statesmen, scholars, editors, professional men, business men and just men were there. His wife, his two sons and his daughter were there. Many of those who were present said that the mind of the thinking world was there, for Booker Washington was regarded as one of the greatest men that ever lived.

Up from Slavery
The Struggle for an Education
Booker T. Washington

One day, while at work in the coal-mine, I happened to overhear two miners talking about a great school for colored people somewhere in Virginia. This was the first time that I had ever heard anything about any kind of school or college that was more pretentious than the little colored school in our town.

In the darkness of the mine I noiselessly crept as close as I could to the two men who were talking. I heard one tell the other that not only was the school established for the members of my race, but that opportunities were provided by which poor but worthy students could work out all or a part of the cost of board, and at the same time be taught some trade or industry.

As they went on describing the school, it seemed to me that it must be the greatest place on earth, and not even Heaven presented more attractions for me at that time than did the Hampton Normal and Agricultural Institute in Virginia, about which these men were talking. I resolved at once to go to that school, although I had no idea where it was, or how many miles away, or how I was going to reach it; I remembered only that I was on fire constantly with one ambition, and that was to go to Hampton. This thought was with me day and night.

After hearing of the Hampton Institute, I continued to work for a few months longer in the coal-mine. While at work there, I heard of a vacant position in the household of General Lewis Ruffner, the owner of the salt-furnace and coal-mine. Mrs. Viola Ruffner, the wife of General Ruffner, was a "Yankee" woman from Vermont. Mrs. Ruffner had a reputation all through the vicinity for being very strict with her servants, and especially with the boys who tried to serve her. Few of them had remained with her more than two or three weeks. They all left with the same excuse: she was too strict. I decided, however, that I would rather try Mrs. Ruffner's house than remain in the coal-mine, and so my mother applied to her for the vacant position. I was hired at a salary of $5 per month.

I had heard so much about Mrs. Ruffner's severity that I was almost afraid to see her, and trembled when I went into her presence. I had not lived with her many weeks, however, before I began to understand her. I soon began to learn that, first of all, she wanted everything kept clean about her, that she wanted things done promptly and systematically, and that at the bottom of everything she wanted absolute honesty and frankness. Nothing must be sloven or slipshod; every door, every fence, must be kept in repair.

I cannot now recall how long I lived with Mrs. Ruffner before going to Hampton, but I think it must have been a year and a half. At any rate, I here repeat what I have said more than once before, that the lessons that I learned in the home of Mrs. Ruffner were as valuable to me as any education I have ever gotten anywhere since. Even to this day I never see bits of paper scattered around a house or in the street that I do not want to pick them up at once. I never see a filthy yard that I do not want to clean it, a paling off of a fence that I do not want to put it on, an unpainted or unwhitewashed house that I do not want to paint or whitewash it, or a button off one's clothes, or a grease-spot on them or on a floor, that I do not want to call attention to it.

From fearing Mrs. Ruffner I soon learned to look upon her as one of my best friends. When she found that she could trust me she did so implicitly. During the one or two winters that I was with her she gave me an opportunity to go to school for an hour in the day during a portion of the winter months, but most of my studying was done at night, sometimes alone, sometimes under someone whom I could hire to teach me. Mrs. Ruffner always encouraged and sympathized with me in all my efforts to get an education. It was while living with her that I began to get together my first library. I secured a dry-goods box, knocked out one side of it, put some shelves in it, and began putting into it every kind of book that I could get my hands upon, and called it "my library."

Without any unusual occurrence I reached Hampton, with a surplus of exactly fifty cents with which to begin my education. To me it had been a long, eventful journey; but the first sight of the large, three-story, brick school building seemed to have rewarded me for all that I had undergone in order to reach the place. If the people who gave the money to provide that building could appreciate the influence the sight of it had upon me, as well as upon thousands of other youths, they would feel all the more encouraged to make such gifts. It seemed to me to be the largest and most beautiful building I had ever seen. The sight of it seemed to give me new life. I felt that a new kind of existence had now begun—that life would now have a new meaning. I felt that I had reached the promised land, and I resolved to let no obstacle prevent me from putting forth the highest effort to fit myself to accomplish the most good in the world.

As soon as possible after reaching the grounds of the Hampton Institute, I presented myself before the head teacher for assignment to a class. Having been so long without proper food, a bath, and change of clothing, I did not, of course, make a very favorable impression upon her, and I could see at once that there were doubts in her mind about the wisdom of admitting me as a student. I felt that I could hardly blame her if she got the idea that I was a worthless loafer or tramp. For some time she did not refuse to admit me, neither did she decide in my favor, and I continued to linger about her, and to impress her in all the ways I could with my worthiness. In the meantime I saw her admitting other students, and that added greatly to my discomfort, for I felt, deep down in my heart, that I could do as well as they, if I could only get a chance to show what was in me.

After some hours had passed, the head teacher said to me, "The adjoining recitation room needs sweeping. Take the broom and sweep it."

It occurred to me at once that here was my chance. Never did I receive an order with more delight. I knew that I could sweep, for Mrs. Ruffner had thoroughly taught me how to do that when I lived with her.

I swept the recitation-room three times. Then I got a dusting-cloth and I dusted it four times. All the woodwork around the walls, every bench, table, and desk, I went over four times with my dusting-cloth. Besides, every piece of furniture had been moved and every closet and corner in the room had been thoroughly cleaned. I had the feeling that in a large measure my future depended upon the impression I made upon the teacher in the cleaning of that room. When I was through, I reported to the head teacher. She was a "Yankee" woman who knew just where to look for dirt. She went into the room and inspected the floor and closets; then she took her handkerchief and rubbed it on the wood-work about the walls, and over the table and benches. When she was unable to find one bit of dirt on the floor, or a particle of dust on any of the furniture, she remarked quietly, "I guess you will do to enter this institution."

Harriet Tubman

The Moses of Her People
1820-1913

About one hundred years ago, people in every civilized country were talking about the "underground railroad" in the United States. The "underground railroad" was not really a railroad under the ground, but a secret way by means of which slaves escaped from their masters in the South and reached free territory. Reaching free territory sometimes meant escape from this country into Canada. Passengers, those seeking to escape to free territory, on the "underground railroad" were led by very brave and daring conductors. Among these conductors there was a woman whose name was Harriet Tubman.

When Harriet was born in Dorchester County, Maryland, in 1820, she was named Araminta Ross. After she grew up, she called herself Harriet. When she became a woman she was married to John Tubman and was called Harriet Tubman.

Harriet almost died with the measles when she was six years old. Soon after she recovered from this, her master threw a heavy weight at her and injured her skull. For years she suffered from pressure on her brain which caused her to fall asleep at any time, wherever she was, whether she was seated on a rail fence or in a chair. It also caused her to stagger sometimes as she walked. No one except her African mother seemed to care for her or to pay any attention to her.

Early one morning a lady came driving up to the home of Harriet's master, who met her at the gate and inquired what he could do for her. She asked for a slave-girl to care for her baby, but offered very low wages. The master shook his head, saying, "I cannot furnish you a girl for that." As the lady pleaded with him, he stood looking on the ground and knitting his brow. Suddenly he lifted his head and said, "Yes, I have just one girl whom you may take; keep your eye on her because she may not have all that is coming to her." Harriet was called, placed in a wagon and driven away to the lady's home.

The first thing the lady gave her to do was to sweep and dust the parlor. Harriet cautiously tiptoed into this wonderfully fine room, amazed at everything she saw. She finally began to sweep in much the same way as she had swept her mother's cabin. As soon as she had finished sweeping, she took the dusting cloth and wiped off the chairs, the table and the mantel-piece. The particles of dust, still flying here and there over the room, soon settled on the furniture again.

About this time, Harriet's new mistress stepped in and began to look around. The dust lay on the table, the chairs and the mantel in such a thick coating that she spoke very harshly to Harriet and ordered her to do the work all over. Harriet swept and dusted just as she had done before. The dust, having no other place to go, settled again on the furniture. The mistress entered the parlor again, bringing with her this time a whip. With this she lashed Harriet with a heavy hand. Five times before breakfast that morning Harriet swept and dusted the parlor.

Just as she had gotten her third whipping, her mistress's sister, who had been awakened from her morning slumber, opened the parlor door. "Why do you whip the child, sister, for not doing what she has never been taught to do?" she asked. "Leave Harriet to me for a few minutes and you will see that she will soon learn how to sweep and dust a room."

The sister ordered Harriet to open the windows first, to sweep the room and leave it a while until the dust settled, and to return then and wipe the dust from the furniture.

Harriet looked strangely at the big window, went to it and raised it inch by inch until it was high enough to fasten by a latch. She set in again and swept, and while the dust was settling, she went out and set the table for breakfast. Then she returned and dusted the parlor.

That night she was ordered to sit up and rock the baby. The baby's cradle and Harriet's chair were placed near her mistress's bed. Occasionally Harriet's eyelids dropped and her head bobbed this way and that way. The cradle kept on rocking because her foot was on the rockers. Once in a great while, the cradle would stop and the baby would begin to cry. The mistress would pick up her whip and give Harriet a cut across the head and shoulders which would make her jump and almost knock the cradle over.

Under such treatment, Harriet became so worn and thin that the lady sent her back to her master saying that she wasn't worth a six-pence. Harriet was turned over to her mother, who nursed her until she was again strong enough to work.

She was then hired out to a man who made her plow, drive oxen, lift a barrel of flour, and sometimes cut a half cord of wood a day. Soon she became ill again. She lay on her sick-bed from Christmas until March. Day after day she prayed, saying, "Oh, Lord, convert old Master; change that man's heart and make him a Christian." When someone told her that as soon as she was able to work, she would be sent away, she changed her prayer, saying: "Lord, if you are never going to change that man's heart, kill him, Lord, and take him out of the way, so he will do no more mischief." Harriet's master finally died but she continued ill for a long time.

Even after she became stronger she still prayed at every turn. When she went to the horse-trough to wash her face and hands, she said, "Lord, wash me and make me clean." When she took the towel to wipe them, she cried, "O Lord, for Jesus' sake, wipe away all my sins." When she took up the broom to sweep, she groaned, "O Lord, whatever sin there is in my heart, sweep it out, Lord, clear and clean."

Early one morning many of the slaves in the "quarters" hurried about with a scared look on their faces, whispering something to each other as they passed. The news had leaked out that Harriet and two of her brothers were to be sold and sent the next day to the far South. As soon as the news reached Harriet, she held a hurried consultation with her brothers, telling them of the terrible things that would befall them if they did not run away to the North. As they stood for a while looking about anxiously and ready to move on, they agreed to start for the North that night.

Harriet began to scratch her head and wonder how she might tell her friends that she was going away. She thought and thought, and finally hit upon the plan of telling them in an old familiar song. As she was passing the next cabin door she sang out:

> *When that old chariot comes,*
> *I'm going to leave you;*
> *I'm bound for the promised land.*
> *Friends, I'm going to leave you.*
>
> *I'm sorry, friends, to leave you,*
> *Farewell! Oh, farewell!*
> *But I'll meet you in the morning!*
> *Farewell! Oh, farewell!*

She looked forward and backward and all around several times. No overseer was in sight. She continued to sing, casting a meaning glance at first one and then another as she passed along:

> *I'll meet you in the morning,*
> *When you reach the promised land,*
> *On the other side of Jordan,*
> *For I'm bound for the promised land.*

That night Harriet and her brothers spoke for a while in a whisper to their father and kissed him good-bye. Without disturbing their dear old mother, each started out quietly in slightly different directions, but all towards the same place. Soon the three came together. The brothers began to say to Harriet in very low tones that they were afraid that old master would send men out for them and capture them. They stood trembling with excitement. All at once, one of them and then the other broke away and ran towards home as fast as they could, falling now and then over a log or a stump. Harriet stood watching them as long as she could see their shadows in the starlight.

Fixing her eye on the North Star, she turned her face in that direction and went forward. All night long she walked until the peep of day, then she lay down in the tall grass in a swamp. She lay there all day. The next night she started out again. Night after night she traveled, occasionally stopping to beg bread. She crouched behind trees or lay concealed in a swamp during the day until she reached Philadelphia.

On her arrival in Philadelphia she stared at the people as they passed. She stood gazing at the fine houses and the streets. She looked at her hands, believing that they, too, looked new. After finding a place to stay, she walked out among the better looking houses and began to ask from door to door if anyone was needed for work. Finally a woman came to the door, opened it just a little way and peeped out as though she were afraid. As Harriet was asking for work, the lady told her to wait a moment while she ran back and pushed her frying-pan further back on the stove. She appeared again at the door, questioned Harriet and then told her to come in.

Harriet walked in and stood listening to the lady's instructions about cleaning. Then she raised the windows and began to sweep. She swept and dusted and cleaned all day. She worked hard the next day and every day until pay-day, when she received her first money. She hid it away with great care and continued her work. The following pay-days she went to the same spot and hid away every penny of her money until she felt that she had enough to go back South.

She gave up her work and traveled night after night until she was again back on the plantation. She hid around among the slaves in their cabins. She whispered to them thrilling stories of the free country, until even women with babies were getting ready to follow her back to the North. After drugging their babies with paregoric and placing them in baskets which they carried on their arms, they set out with "Moses", as they called her, for the free country.

They forded rivers, climbed mountains, went through the swamps, threaded the forests with their feet sore and often bleeding. They traveled during the night and kept in hiding during the day. One of the men fell by the wayside. Harriet took out her pistol, and pointing it at his head, said, "Dead men tell no tales; you go on or die!" He arose trembling and dragged along with the party until they reached the North.

As soon as Harriet had landed this party, she began working again and making preparations to go back on her next trip. One night she went back to the plantation, secured a horse and a two-wheel cart and drove away with her aged mother and father. After placing them on the train, she traveled in the cart night after night until she made her way through

Maryland to Wilmington, Delaware, where she had sent her parents.

As soon as the three of them met in Wilmington, Harriet took her parents to a well-known underground railroad station. This was simply the home of a Quaker friend. He gave them food and shelter and each a new pair of shoes. He furnished Harriet with money to take her parents on to Canada, and kept the horse and cart for sale. Harriet and her parents went on, making their way with difficulty, until they reached Canada.

Harriet remained in Canada for a short time only, then slipped back among the plantation cabins in Maryland. Again and again she went back—nineteen times—leading away in the darkness, in all, over three hundred slaves. The slave masters of that region in Maryland, whence so many were being stolen away, after trying hard to catch Harriet, offered a reward of $40,000 for her, dead or alive. They posted such a notice in all public places.

After fifteen years of such adventure, Harriet bought a little home place near Auburn, N.Y., and settled on it with her dear old parents. Frequently responding to a knock at the door, she arose and found that someone had brought to her a poor, old, homeless person. Without hesitating to ask many questions, she took in every one of them until she had twenty old people, for whom she worked and sought support.

William H. Seward, Governor of New York, once said to her when she went to him for aid, "Harriet, you have worked for others long enough. If you would ever ask anything for yourself, I would gladly give it to you but I will not help you to rob yourself for others any longer."

Many years after that, Governor Seward died, and a large number of persons gathered at his funeral. Many very beautiful flowers were received by his family on that sad occasion. On the day of the funeral, just before the coffin was closed, a woman as black as night stole quietly in and laid a wreath of field flowers at his feet and as quietly glided out again. Friends of the family whispered, "It's the Governor's friend, Harriet."

Harriet continued to work and take in homeless old people until the outbreak of the Civil War. At that time, Governor Andrew of Massachusetts sent for her. He asked if she would go South as a spy and a scout, and if need be, a hospital nurse for the Union soldiers. She stood thinking for a moment, then said that she would go. He bade her return home and be ready at a moment's notice. Harriet left his office and returned to Auburn. She went about asking friends to look out for the old people in her home while she was away.

Soon after she reached home, a messenger arrived with orders for her to report immediately. She hastily grabbed a few necessary things, kissed her parents, saying good-bye to them and to the inmates of the home, and hurried away to join the company of soldiers on its way south. They traveled several days. As soon as they arrived, Harriet was ordered to act as a scout and a spy for the soldiers. She took charge and led them through the jungle and the swamp. She approached the frightened slaves, often gaining valuable information from them. She stood in the battle-line when the shots were falling like hail and the bodies of dead and wounded men were dropping like leaves in autumn.

Being called upon to nurse the soldiers in the hospitals, she extracted from roots and herbs what she called a healing substance. As she went to a sick soldier and felt his burning forehead, she often poured out a spoonful of her medicine and placed it in his mouth. After a few days of such treatment frequently a soldier smiled at her and thanked her.

She often bathed the wounds of soldiers from early morning until late at night. She nursed many with smallpox. Occasionally, after a long day's toil, she went to her little cabin and made fifty pies, several pans of ginger-bread and two casks of root-beer. One of the men went through the camps selling these things for her. Almost as soon as she obtained the money from the sale of them she mailed it on to her old parents for the support of their home.

Once while Harriet was on this trip she went with some gunboats up the Combahee River. The frightened slaves along the way left their work and took to the woods. Some of those who fled peeped out from behind trees at the gunboats and ran away like deer when they heard the sound of the steam whistle. One old man said, "Well, Master said the Yankees had horns and tails but I never believed it till now." Eight hundred of these people were taken on board the gunboats to be carried to Beaufort, S.C. Some of them before going aboard grabbed from the fire and placed on their heads pails of smoking rice. Others had on their backs a bag with a pig in it; and some carried two pigs in their bags.

Soon after this trip Harriet returned to her little home place, which was about to be sold to pay off a mortgage. A friend, the daughter of a professor of Auburn Theological Seminary, hearing of Harriet's trouble, came to see her. Harriet greeted her friend as usual and invited her to sit down; she too sat down and began to tell about the war. Her friend listened for a long, long time but finally interrupted her to ask about the home and the mortgage. Harriet, concealing nothing from her, told her the exact conditions of the mortgage.

The friend suggested the idea of having her life story written as a means of getting money to pay off the mortgage. Harriet nodded her head in full agreement with what her friend was proposing and asked if she would write the story. The friend counted aloud the days before the mortgage had to be paid off and, realizing that they were not many, set herself at once to the task of writing the story of Harriet's life.

Harriet sat with her friend day after day, each time telling of some incident in her life which she had not told before. The story was finally finished and published, and from the proceeds of it the mortgage was paid off.

Harriet worked hard, saying all the time that she wished to free the home of debt so that she might give it to her race to be used as an Old Folks' Home. When the property was almost free of debt and there were twenty aged women in the home, she went among them with a smile dividing the little she had, until she was stricken with pneumonia and died.

Following her death, the Harriet Tubman Club of New York City, together with the whole Empire State Federation of Negro Women's Clubs, erected to her memory a handsome monument. This monument is in the form of a shaft. One of the principal designs on this shaft is in the form of three oak logs out of which flowers are growing.

The citizens of Auburn held a memorial meeting for her at the Auditorium Theatre. Booker T. Washington, the mayor and the ex-mayor of Auburn were the speakers on that occasion. The lower floor of the theatre was filled and every box was occupied. In one box sat a group of Civil War veterans and in another sat the leading society women of Auburn. On the stage sat the Auburn Festival Chorus and Orchestra and the guests.

In the presence of this audience, Harriet Tubman's grand-niece unveiled a large bronze tablet the gift of the citizens of Auburn to the memory of Harriet Tubman. In accepting this tablet, the mayor of the city said, "In recognition of Harriet Tubman's unselfish devotion to the cause of humanity, the city of Auburn accepts this tablet dedicated to her memory."

The tablet was placed in the county court-house with the following inscription:

IN MEMORY OF
HARRIET TUBMAN

Born a slave in Maryland about 1821
Died in Auburn, N. Y., March 10, 1913

Called the "Moses" of her people during the Civil War. With rare courage, she led over 300 Negroes up from slavery to freedom, and rendered invaluable service as nurse and spy.

With implicit trust in God, she braved every danger and overcame every obstacle; withal she possessed extraordinary foresight and judgment, so that she truthfully said, "On my underground railroad I never ran my train off the track and I never lost a passenger."

Blanche Kelso Bruce

Senator—Register of the U.S. Treasury
1841-1898

On the first day of March, in the year 1841, a little slave boy started out from Farmville, Virginia, on a journey. The strange thing about it was, he did not know where he was going or how long the journey would take. However, he started out and traveled west and south and east and north for fifty-seven long years.

After his first few years of experience on the road, he reached Brunswick, Missouri. The manager of a little printing office in the town offered him a job which attracted him. He accepted it and remained in Brunswick some years, assisting on a printing-press as a "printer's devil".

At the noon hour, one day, he sat with his head buried in a newspaper. Someone said, as he slapped Bruce on the back, "Hello, Branch, what are you doing way out here?" Bruce seemed greatly surprised to hear someone call him Branch, for he had long ago changed his name to Blanche. He raised his head and looked all around but did not see any one, and so he went on with his reading. After a short time, "flap" went a sound. Something had slapped him on the back of his neck.

He jumped up and looked around but still did not see any one. Then he said in a loud voice, "Who are you, anyhow? Stop slapping me." And with that, he sat down again.

A little shrill voice answered, "Yes, you are out here working on a printing-press. I've been following you. You came all the way from Virginia. What do you know about a printing-press? In the early days no one at all could do any printing in your state, because the state did not allow it."

Blanche Bruce scowled and frowned and looked all around but did not see any one. And so he shouted out, "Oh hush! I've been reading all about printing. In the early days none of the American colonies encouraged printing. Some of the printers were even arrested for printing. For thirty years Cambridge, Massachusetts, was the only place in America where printing was done, and that was controlled by the Government. Now, you shut up!" After that, he arose and went in to begin his work.

For years, Bruce says, he heard no more of the little voice, but he could not forget that experience. In spite of it, he worked in Brunswick until he decided to move on to Lawrence, Kansas. By this time, of course, he had grown a great deal in height and size. His love for books had not waned, and his experience in the Civil War had taught him a great deal.

Seeing that the few Negro children in Lawrence were ignorant, he opened a school for them, but finding later that there were more children in Hannibal, Missouri, who needed a school, he went there and began teaching.

Bruce kept on thinking and moving until one day, in the year 1866, he found himself at Oberlin, Ohio, sawing wood. "Whew! I am so tired, I believe I'll sit down on this log and rest a while," he said to himself, as he wiped the perspiration from his forehead with his hand. No sooner had he sat down, than "flap" went something across his back. He jumped up, looked all around and said to himself, "That's strange!"

"Yes, it is strange," said a little shrill voice, "but I've been following you all the time. I hear you are out here sawing wood to keep yourself in Oberlin College. Just keep at it."

Bruce seemed really disturbed now, for this voice sounded exactly like that one in Brunswick, Missouri, years before. Said he in a gruff voice, "I don't know what you are, but get on away or I'll saw you." He finished his sawing that day and sawed many more days before the end of the college year.

In company with other students who were going to their homes for the summer, he left Oberlin College bound for some place, he really did not know where. By some means he continued to travel, and finally found himself working on a big vessel which ran between Council Bluffs, Iowa, and St. Louis, Missouri. One day, after his vessel was anchored at St. Louis, he secured a newspaper and sat down to his old trade. He read and read and finally came across an article which told how badly Mississippi was needing educated men. Many of her men had been killed in the war, and until more food was raised there was really little left for the people to eat. Bruce read some parts of the article a second time, and while he sat there, decided to start for Mississippi as soon as he could.

The way soon opened, and after some days of travel, he found himself in Mississippi. Mississippi seemed to need him badly. Very soon, the military Governor-General of that State appointed him to take charge of the election in a whole county. The name of that county was Tallahatchie. He traveled over it from town to town, making speeches and influencing men, until after the election. Within a year, he met the Mississippi Legislature at Jackson and was elected as Sergeant-at-arms in the Senate. In this position, he assisted in many ways the one who presided over the Senate. If anyone in the Senate was disorderly, he arrested him.

Bruce kept on traveling until the Governor of Mississippi noticed him and appointed him as Tax Assessor of Bolivar County. He had to determine how much taxes the people in that county should pay. He afterwards stepped into the position of Sheriff and Tax Collector, and then Superintendent of Schools of that county. Before leaving Bolivar County, he bought a plantation.

Blanche Kelso Bruce had been traveling for over thirty years now. The greatest milestone in his journey, he said to a friend one day, was now in sight. The State of Mississippi had elected him to represent her in the United States Senate at Washington, D.C. He knew little about the customs in the Senate, but one day he found himself sitting in the Senate

Chamber ready to receive what was called his induction into office.

Something within him, which sounded just as plainly as the shrill voice at Oberlin had sounded, seemed to say, "You will have no one to escort you up the aisle like the other new senators have; but you have traveled all the way from Farmville, Virginia, as a slave, to Washington, D.C., as a senator, so go right ahead."

Senator Bruce straightened up and said to himself, "Ah! I guess that's the something within me that has been following me all these years. It's my turn to go up now, and I am going."

When he had gotten about half way up the aisle, a tall gentleman touched him on the arm. He stood for a moment as if he were dreaming or as if he were listening to the shrill voice again. But no, this was a real man who said to him, "Excuse me, Mr. Bruce, I did not until this moment see that you were without an escort. Permit me. My name is Conkling." He linked his arm in that of Senator Bruce and they marched up to the desk and back to their seats together.

It was this man, Senator Roscoe Conkling of New York, who assisted Senator Bruce in gaining the chairmanship of one committee in the Senate and in securing a place on other committees. A few years later, when a son was born to Senator and Mrs. Bruce, he was named Roscoe Conkling Bruce, in honor of the Senator.

Although, as he had said, the greatest milestone in his journey had been reached, and he had served in the Senate for six years, the journey was not yet completed. He went on and became Register of the United States Treasury.

One morning, as he sat in his office looking at a five-dollar bill, some one seemed to shake him. He looked up but there was nobody in the room but him. He said that he thought he had simply made a mistake, but soon something within that sounded just like the little shrill voice of bygone days seemed to say, "You've been a pretty good traveler. Here you are again. I hear that not a single paper dollar can be issued unless the name 'B.K. Bruce, Register of the Treasury', is stamped in the lower left-hand corner of it."

Mr. Bruce now leaned back and laughed out right, "Ha! ha! ha!" He seemed to realize that all these years no voice outside of his inner self had been talking to him.

He served in the position of Register of the Treasury for four years, then retired to private life as a platform lecturer. Later, he entered upon his duties as Recorder of Deeds of the District of Columbia and as a trustee of the Washington Public Schools. The end of his long fifty-seven-year journey, which came March 17, 1898, found him as Register of the United States Treasury for a second time.

Benjamin Banneker

Astronomer and Surveyor
1732-1804

I
Childhood

One winter evening long ago, everything in Baltimore County, Maryland, was covered with deep snow. Icicles nearly a foot long hung from the roofs of the rough log cabins. The trees of the thick forest which extended for miles around stood like silent ghosts in the stillness, for no one in all that wooded country stirred out on such an evening.

Far away from the other cabins stood the Banneker cabin. Little Benjamin Banneker was busy before a glowing wood fire roasting big, fat chestnuts in the hot embers. His grandmother sat in the corner in a quaint split-bottom, white-oak chair, knitting and telling him about her native country, England.

She said, "When I was in England, milking the cows on a cattle farm was a part of my daily duties. One day I was accused of stealing a pail of milk which had in fact been kicked over by the cow. Instead of meting out a more severe punishment, the officers of the law sentenced me to be shipped to America. Being unable to pay for my passage, I was sold, upon my arrival in America, to a tobacco planter on the Patapsco River to serve a period of seven years to pay the cost of my passage."

Silence reigned for a few moments, then she continued, "I worked out my period of service, then bought a part of the farm on which I had worked. I also bought two African slaves from a ship in the Chesapeake Bay. One of the slaves, your grandfather, the son of an African king, had been stolen from the coast of Africa."

Little Benjamin then asked, pointing to his grandfather, who was sitting on the other side of the hearth, "Was grandfather that man, grandmother?"

"Yes," she said. She continued her story, ending with a beautiful description of the River Thames, the Tower of London, and Westminster Abbey.

All was still for a while, except for the occasional moving of Benjamin and the bursting of chestnuts. Benjamin's grandfather, who was sitting with his eyes closed, now broke the silence. Said he, "Benjamin, what are you going to be when you are a man, a *chestnut* roaster?"

"I am going to be—I am going to be—what is it, grandmother? You know you told me a story about the man who knew all the stars," said Benjamin.

"An astronomer," replied his grandmother.

"That's it, I am going to be an astronomer," answered Benjamin.

"You have changed in the last day or two, then," said his grandfather. "The day your grandmother told you about the man who could figure so well with his head, you said you would be that,"

"That man was a born mathematician," suggested his grandmother.

Benjamin began to blink his eyelids rapidly and to twist and turn for an answer. Soon his mouth flew open saying, "Well, I'll be both, I'll be both!"

His grandmother interrupted by saying, "I wonder what has become of my little inventor? Benjamin, you remember what you said when I told you the story about that inventor."

Benjamin gave that look which always said, "Well, I am caught"; but soon he recovered and with this reply, "I can tell you what I am going to do, I am going to school first to learn to figure. And then while I am farming a little for my living I can stay up at night and watch the stars. And in the afternoon I can study and invent things until I am tired, and then I can go out and watch my bees."

"When are you going to sleep, my boy?" asked his grandmother.

"In the morning," said he.

"And you are going to have a farm and bees, too?" she asked.

"Yes, grandmother," said Benjamin, "we might just as well have something while we are here. Father says that he will never take mother and me to his native country—Africa—to live. Grandmother, did you and grandfather have any children besides mother?"

"Yes, there were three other children," replied his grandmother.

"When father and mother were married," said Benjamin, "mother didn't change her name at all from Mary Banneker as the ladies do now, but father changed his name to Robert Banneker. I am glad of it, for you see you are Banneker, grandfather is

Banneker, I am Banneker and all of us are Bannekers now."

"My boy," interrupted his grandfather, "I am waiting to hear how you are going to buy a farm."

"Oh, grandfather," said Benjamin as he arose, "you remember that mother and father gave Mr. Gist seven thousand pounds of tobacco and Mr. Gist gave them one hundred acres of land here in Baltimore County. Grandfather, don't you think father will give me some of this land? He cannot use it all."

"Yes, when you are older, Benjamin. But you must go to school and learn to read first," answered his grandfather.

"Yes but—ouch, that coal is hot!" cried Benjamin as he shook his hand, danced about the floor and buried his fingers in a pillow. That time he had picked up a hot coal instead of a chestnut. Sometime after his fingers were "doctored" and he was apparently snug in bed for the night, he shook his hands and cried out for his grandmother.

Benjamin rose the next morning, and after breakfast, began again to roast chestnuts. Morning after morning he roasted chestnuts until the snow had all cleared away. Then he entered a pay school and soon learned to read, write and do some arithmetic. After some months had passed he began to borrow books and to study by himself.

II
Farmer and Mathematician

When Benjamin was about twenty-seven, his father died. As he had prophesied when he was a boy, his father's farm bought with the tobacco, became his. On this farm was Banneker's house—a log cabin about half a mile from the Patapsco River. In his doorway he often stood looking at the near and distant beautiful hills along the banks of this river. What he said about his bees when he was a boy came true also. These he kept in his orchard; and in the midst of this orchard a spring which never failed, babbled beneath a large golden willow tree. His beautiful garden and his well-kept grounds seemed to give him pleasure.

Banneker never married, but lived alone in retirement after the death of his mother. He cooked his own food and washed his own clothes. All who knew him, and especially those who saw that he was a genius, spoke well of him. He always greeted his visitors cheerfully, and he kept a book in which was written the name of every person by whose visit he felt greatly honored.

Someone who knew him well says that he was a brave-looking, pleasant man with something very noble in his face. He was large and somewhat stout. In his old age he wore a broad-brimmed hat which covered his thick suit of white hair. He always wore a superfine, drab broad cloth coat with a straight collar and long waist coat. His manners, someone says, were those of a perfect gentleman—kind, generous, hospitable, dignified, pleasing, very modest and unassuming.

He worked on his farm for his living, but found time to study all the books which he could borrow. He studied the Bible, history, biography, travels, romance, and other books, but his greatest interest was in mathematics. Like many other scholars of his day, he often amused himself during his leisure by solving hard problems. Scholars from many parts of the country often sent him difficult problems. It is said that he solved every one sent to him and he often sent in return an original question in rhyme. For example, he sent the following question to Mr. George Ellicott, which was solved by a scholar of Alexandria:

A Cooper and Vintner sat down for a talk,
Both being so groggy, that neither could walk.
Says Cooper to Vintner, "I'm the first of my trade;
There's no kind of vessel but what I have made.
And of any shape, Sir—just what you will;
And of any size, Sir—from a ton to a gill!"
"Then", says the Vintner, "you're the man for me—
Make me a vessel, if we can agree.
The top and the bottom diameter define,
To bear that proportion as fifteen to nine;
Thirty-five inches are just what I crave,
No more and no less, in the depth will I have.
Just thirty-nine gallons this vessel must hold,
Then I will reward you with silver and gold.
Give me your promise, my honest old friend?"
"I'll make it to-morrow, that you may depend!"

So the next day the Cooper his work to discharge,
Soon made the new vessel, but made it too large;
He took out some staves, which made it too small,
And then cursed the vessel, the Vintner and all.
He beat on his breast, "By the Powers!" he swore
He never would work at his trade any more!
Now, my worthy friend, find out, if you can,
The vessel's dimensions and comfort the man.

III

Inventor and Astronomer

When Banneker was about thirty-eight years old he sat day after day working on a clock. Finally he finished it with his imperfect tools and with only a borrowed watch for a model. He had never seen a clock for there was not one, it is said, within fifty miles of him. An article published in London, England, in 1864, says that Banneker's clock was probably the first clock every part of which was made in America. For many hours and days he turned and adjusted the hands of his clock until they moved smoothly and the clock struck on the hour.

Time passed, and after some years Mr. George Ellicott's family—Quakers from Pennsylvania they were—began to build flour-mills, a store and a post-office in a valley adjoining Banneker's farm. Banneker was now fifty-five years old, and had won the reputation of knowing more than any other person in that county. Mr. Ellicott opened his library to him. He gave him a book which told of the stars. He gave him tables about the moon. He urged him to work out problems for almanacs.

Early every evening Banneker wrapped himself in a big cloak, stretched out upon the ground and lay there all night looking at the stars and planets. At sunrise he rose and went to his house. He slept and rested all the morning and worked in the afternoon. His neighbors peeped through the cracks of his house one morning and saw him resting. They began at once to call him a lazy fellow who would come to no good end.

In spite of this, he compiled an almanac. His first almanac was published for the year 1792. It so interested one of the great men of the country that he wrote to two almanac publishers of Baltimore about it. These publishers gladly published Banneker's almanac. They said that it was the work of a genius, and that it met the hearty approval of distinguished astronomers.

Banneker wrote Thomas Jefferson, then Secretary of State, on behalf of his people, and sent him one of his almanacs. Mr. Jefferson replied:

Philadelphia, August 30, 1791.

Sir—I thank you sincerely for your letter of the 19th inst. and for the almanac it contained. Nobody wishes more than I do to see such proofs as you exhibit, that nature has given to your race talents equal to those of the other races of men.

I am with great esteem, Sir,

Your most obedient servant,
THOS. JEFFERSON

IV
Surveyor

This strange man, Benjamin Banneker, never went away from home any distance until he was fifty-seven years old. Then he was asked by the commissioners, appointed to run the boundary lines of the District of Columbia, to go with them. He accompanied them.

Later, *The Evening Star*, a Washington daily paper, said, "Major L'Enfant, the engineer, bossed the job while Benjamin Banneker did the work."

On Banneker's return home from Washington he told his friends that during that trip he had not touched strong drink, his one temptation. "For," said he, "I feared to trust myself even with wine, lest it should steal away the little sense I had." In those days wines and liquors were upon the tables of the best families.

Perhaps no one alive today knows the exact day of Banneker's death. In the fall, probably of 1804, on a beautiful day, he walked out on the hills apparently seeking the sunlight as a tonic. While walking, he met a neighbor to whom he told his condition. He and his neighbor walked along slowly to his house. He lay down at once upon his couch, became speechless and died.

During a previous illness he had asked that all his papers, almanacs, and the like, be given at his death to Mr. Ellicott. Just two days after his death and while he was being buried, his house burned to the ground. It burned so rapidly that the clock and all his papers were destroyed. A feather bed on which he had slept for many years was removed at his death. The sister to whom he gave it opened it some years later and in it was found a purse of money.

Benjamin Banneker was well known on two continents. An article written about him in 1864 by a member of the London Emancipation Society says, "Though no monument marks the spot where he was born and lived a true and high life and was buried, yet history must record that the most original scientific intellect which the South has yet produced was that of the African, Benjamin Banneker."

Benjamin Banneker

Benjamin Banneker was born in the State of Maryland, in the year 1732, of pure African parentage; their blood never having been corrupted by the introduction of a drop of Anglo-Saxon. His father was a slave, and of course could do nothing towards the education of the child. The mother, however, being free, succeeded in purchasing the freedom of her husband, and they, with their son, settled on a few acres of land, where Benjamin remained during the lifetime of his parents. His entire schooling was gained from an obscure country school, established for the education of the children of free negroes; and these advantages were poor, for the boy appears to have finished studying before he arrived at his fifteenth year.

Although out of school, Banneker was still a student, and read with great care and attention such books as he could get. Mr. George Ellicott, a gentlemen of fortune and considerable literary taste, and who resided near to Benjamin, became interested in him, and lent him books from his large library. Among these books were three on Astronomy. A few old and imperfect astronomical instruments also found their way into the boy's hands, all of which he used with great benefit to his own mind.

Banneker took delight in the study of the languages, and soon mastered the Latin, Greek and German. He was also proficient in the French. The classics were not neglected by him, and the general literary knowledge which he possessed caused Mr. Ellicott to regard him as the most learned man in the town, and he never failed to introduce Banneker to his most distinguished guests.

About this time Benjamin turned his attention particularly to astronomy, and determined on making calculations for an almanac, and completed a set for the whole year. Encouraged by this attempt, he entered upon calculations for subsequent years, which, as well as the former, he began and finished without the least assistance from any person or books than those already mentioned; so that whatever merit is attached to his performance is exclusively his own.

He published an almanac in Philadelphia for the years 1792, '93, '94, and '95, which contained his calculations, exhibiting the different aspects of the planets, a table of the motions of the sun and moon, their risings and settings, and the courses of the bodies of the planetary system. By this time Banneker's acquirements had become generally known, and the best scholars in the country opened correspondence with him. Goddard & Angell, the well-known Baltimore publishers, engaged his pen for their establishment, and became the publishers of his almanacs.

He knew every branch of history, both natural and civil; he had read all the original historians of England, France, and was a great antiquarian. With such a fund of knowledge his conversation was equally interesting, instructive, and entertaining. Banneker was so favorably appreciated by the first families in Virginia, that in 1803 he was invited by Mr. Jefferson, then President of the United States, to visit him at Monticello, where the statesman had gone for recreation. But he was too infirm to undertake the journey. He died the following year, aged seventy-two. Like the golden sun that has sunk beneath the western horizon, but still throws upon the world, which he sustained and enlightened in his career, the reflected beams of his departed genius, his name can only perish with his language.

Phillis Wheatley

First Poetess of Her Race on American Soil
1753-1784

In 1753 a baby girl was born on the Western Coast of Africa. Her mother did not sit for hours making beautiful little dresses and doing embroidery for her, for that is not the custom in Africa. Babies do not need many clothes in that warm country. There little children, and grown people too, run around with just a piece of cloth tied about their waists.

The child was not robust, but she grew and grew until she soon became her mother's companion. Her mother, believing that a Great Spirit lives in the sun, went out of her little thatched-roof house every morning and prostrated herself to pour out water before the rising sun. The child often watched the water as it streamed down, and sometimes she jumped and clapped her little hands with glee.

One bright morning, after this religious ceremony was performed and breakfast was over, the girl ran out to play with the other children. She was shedding her front teeth, but she was not large for her age and she was none too strong. While she and her playmates

140

were having a happy time, suddenly one of the older children exclaimed, "Hoi! hoi!" Every child looked up and took to its heels. There were strange-looking men hurrying towards them. The children ran and screamed. Our little girl stumbled and fell, and the man, pursuing her, grabbed her. She kicked and yelled but he held her fast. Her best friend ran behind a big tree, but she, too, was caught. They both kicked and yelled, but they were taken on board an American vessel. Other children who were caught were also brought to the shore kicking and crying.

When there were almost enough of them for a boat-load, the vessel sailed away. They were on the water for many days. The voyage was long and the sea was rough. The waters lashed the sides of the vessel as it rocked to and fro. Some of the children fell to the floor with spells of vomiting. Many a night everything for a time was in complete darkness and everybody was afraid. The little vessel, however, tugged away for days and nights until it sighted lights flickering in the Boston Harbor. All the voyagers, tired and hungry and lonely, rejoiced to be nearing even an unknown land. Soon the boat pulled into the harbor, and although no comforts had been provided for them for the night, weariness of body so overcame loneliness of heart that all of them soon fell asleep.

The news had gone abroad in Boston that a shipload of Africans was approaching. The next morning many Bostonians hurried to the harbor to see the Africans. Among the number of spectators there was a Mrs. John Wheatley, the wife of a tailor. She walked around and looked many of the African girls over from head to foot. Finally she handed the shipmaster money and took our girl away with her to her home.

She and her daughter were busy for a while heating kettles of water, getting out clothing and sewing on a button here and there, preparatory to giving her a good hot bath. When the child was called in she gazed at this strange-looking object which Mrs. Wheatley called a tub. She looked at the soap and felt it. She stretched her eyes as she looked upon the nice white clothes on the chair. She seemed just a little afraid and yet she did as Mrs. Wheatley told her and soon had her bath.

After she was dressed, she met another big surprise. She was taken into a dining-room, where the table was all spread with white linen. There were strange-looking things to eat. She began eating, but said that the food did not taste like the food in Africa. She picked over this and picked over that, but nothing tasted just right. Nevertheless she smiled, and it appeared that she was not very hungry. Mrs. Wheatley watched her closely as she came in touch with all of these strange new things and assured her that in a few days everything would not seem so queer. The girl adopted the customs of the family and they named her Phillis Wheatley.

Every day as Mrs. Wheatley's daughter sat reading or writing letters, Phillis stood looking at her in wonder. Miss Wheatley seemed to write with so much ease that one day Phillis went out with a piece of charcoal in her hand and began to try to write on the side of a wall. Miss Wheatley, who was seated at a window, watched her for a long time, then called her in and showed her how to make some letters. Phillis busied herself for the remainder of the day making letters and keeping Miss Wheatley busy showing her how to make new ones. That night she scarcely wished to leave her writing to go to bed, but Miss Wheatley persuaded her by promising to give her a lesson every day. They set the lesson hour and Phillis went to bed smiling and shaking with joy. Just at the right time every day she walked into Miss Wheatley's room for her lesson. When her lessons were over and she was not busy with her work, she was poring over her books. In less than a year and a half she could easily read the most difficult parts of the Bible without making a mistake. In four years people in different parts of the country began to hear of her and write to her and even furnish her with books. To the surprise of the Wheatleys, she was soon studying and reading the Latin language without any one to help her.

At the age of fourteen, Phillis began to write poetry. Often when some great person of whom she knew died, she would write a poem to commemorate his death. Sometimes she awoke during the night and composed verses but could not recall all of them the next morning. As soon as Mrs. Wheatley discovered this, she began leaving a light and writing materials on the table at Phillis's bedside every night. In cold weather, she always left a fire burning on the hearth in Phillis's room.

For six years Phillis was busy writing poetry and letters and studying and receiving visitors. Many people in England corresponded with her. The educated people of Boston were often seen making their way to the Wheatley home. They talked with Phillis and questioned her, and often asked her to read some of her poetry. When she in turn went to their homes they took great pride in showing her off as a wonder. Those who talked with her marveled at her knowing so much about English poetry, astronomy, ancient history and the Bible.

She continued to write and study. In her nineteenth year she became so thin and pale that the family doctor advised Mrs. Wheatley to give her a sea voyage. Accordingly, the following summer, Phillis set out for London with Mrs. Wheatley's son, who was going there on business. On her arrival in London, after days of travel, some of her friends with whom she had corresponded, met her and welcomed her. As she visited the different ones, she went to dinner parties and theatre parties given in her honor.

When articles about her poetry began to appear in many of the leading London papers, her friends advised her to have all of her poems published. She considered the matter and went with some of them to see a publisher. After reviewing the poems, the publisher accepted them and published them, in 1773, under the title, "Poems on Various Subjects, Religious and Moral, by Phillis Wheatley".

As soon as copies of the poems reached America and were read, many people expressed doubt about the author being an African girl. The Governor of Massachusetts and seventeen other Bostonians, upon hearing this report, wrote a letter assuring people everywhere that these poems were written by Phillis Wheatley.

Phillis Wheatley's London friends were making plans to present her to their king, George III, who was expected in London within a few days, but word reached her that Mrs. Wheatley was quite ill and wished to see her at once. Her passage was secured for her while she packed her trunk. As fortune would have it, a vessel was sailing that day for Boston. She bade her friends good-bye and put out to sea. The vessel moved slowly, but after days of travel it landed at Boston. She was met at the dock and hurried to the Wheatley home. Mrs. Wheatley caressed her again and again, and lay looking at her for days. For two months Phillis waited upon Mrs. Wheatley and sat by her bedside night after night until she died. Four years later another shock came to the family—Mr. Wheatley died. Seven months after his death his daughter passed away, leaving Phillis alone.

Phillis lived a short while with a friend of the Wheatleys and then rented a room and lived alone. She lived in this way until she began to taste the bitterness of Revolutionary War times. At that time one goose sold for forty dollars and one-fourth of a lamb sold for fifty dollars.

One evening during these hard times she met a handsome man by the name of Peters, who wore a wig and carried a cane. He also kept a grocery store, practiced law and wrote poetry. He began at once to pay court to Phillis. Later he called on her, often took her out for a stroll or to a party until they were married several weeks later.

After the wedding day, Phillis began her daily round of sweeping and cleaning, cooking and washing and ironing. As the years came and went, three children came into their lives. Mr. Peters failed in business and then left to Phillis the support of herself and the children. She secured a job in a cheap boarding-house, where she worked every day from early morning until late at night. She became ill from overwork.

During the first summer of her illness two of her children died. The following winter, cold and snowy, some charitable organization placed in her backyard a load of wood. Although the wood lay there, Peters often went out, leaving Phillis lying on her poor bed without a spark of fire on the hearth. She lay there for weeks.

Friends and distant relatives of the Wheatleys often inquired about Phillis, but no one seemed to know where she was. Finally one December afternoon, in 1784, as a grand-niece of Mrs. Wheatley chanced to be walking up Court Street in Boston she met a funeral. Upon inquiry she learned that it was the funeral of Phillis Wheatley.

AN HYMN TO THE MORNING

Attend my lays, ye ever-honor'd nine;
Assist my labours, and my strain refine;
In smoothest numbers pour the notes along,
For bright aurora now demands my song.

Aurora hail, and all the thousand dyes,
Which deck thy progress through the vaulted skies:
The morn awakes, and wide extends her rays,
On ev'ry leaf the gentle zephyr plays;
Harmonious lays the feather'd race resume,
Part the bright eye, and shake the painted plume.

Ye shady groves, your verdant gloom display
To shield your poet from the burning day;
Calliope awake the sacred lyre,
While thy fair sisters fan the pleasing fire:
The bow'rs, the gales, the variegated skies
In all their pleasures in my bosom rise.

Phillis Wheatley

See in the East th' illustrious king of day!
His rising radiance drives the shades away.
But oh! I feel his fervid beams too strong,
And scarce begun, concludes th' abortive song.

—From Poems on Various Subjects,
Religious and Moral.

AN HYMN TO THE EVENING

Soon as the sun forsook the eastern main
The pealing thunder shook the heav'nly plain;
Majestic grandeur! From the zephyr's wing,
Exhales the incense of the blooming spring.
Soft purl the streams, the birds renew their notes,
And through the air their mingled music floats,

Through all the heav'ns what beauteous dyes are
     spread!
But the west glories in the deepest red;
So may our breasts with ev'ry virtue glow
The living temples of our God below!
Fill'd with the praise of him who gives the light,
And draws the sable curtains of the night,

Let placid slumbers sooth each weary mind,
At morn to wake more heav'nly, more refin'd.
So shall the labours of the day begin
More pure, more guarded from the snares of sin.

149

Night's leaden sceptre seals my drowsy eyes,
Then cease, my song, till fair Aurora rise.

Imagination! Who can sing thy force?
Or who describe the swiftness of thy course?
Soaring through air to find the bright abode,
Th' empyreal palace of the thund'ring God,
We on thy pinions can surpass the wind,
And leave the rolling universe behind:
From star to star the mental optics rove,
Measure the skies, and range the realms above.
There in one view we grasp the mighty whole,
Or with new worlds amaze th' unbounded soul.
                                   —*Taken from "Imagination"*

Improve your privileges while they stay,
Ye pupils, and each hour redeem, that bears
Or good or bad report of you to heav'n;
Let sin, that baneful evil to the soul,
By you be shunn'd, nor once remit your guard;
Suppress the deadly serpent in its egg,
Ye blooming plants of human race divine,
An Ethiop tells you 'tis your greatest foe;
Its transient sweetness turns to endless pain,
And in immense perdition sinks the soul.
                          —*Taken from "To the University of*
                              Cambridge, in New England"

Josiah Henson

The Faithful Servant
1789-1881

Josiah Henson, or "Si" as he was called, tried at the age of fifteen to out-hoe, out-reap, out-husk, out-dance every other boy on his master's plantation in Charles County, Maryland. Boys would sometimes stand around and look at "Si" and talk about the wonderful things he could do and the great stories they had heard about him. One special story they liked to tell.

The story was this: As a child "Si" was such a sickly little fellow his master offered to sell him cheaply to the man who owned his mother. His mother's master hesitated to buy him, saying, "I am afraid the little devil might die. I do not wish to buy a dead brat." Nevertheless, he finally agreed to shoe some horses for Si's master and thus pay a small sum for Si.

Occasionally after some boy was through telling this stock tale, which always produced a laugh, other boys would begin to guess why Si was so great. One said one day, "I guess it's that meat Si eats at

Christmas time. He certainly doesn't get much at any other time."

"No," said another, who slept in the cabin with Si, "Si sleeps more soundly than any one of us in the cabin, and there are twelve of us who sleep in that one room, counting the women and girls. Give me a board and let me show you how Si stretches out on his plank. Now give me some straw to go under my head. How I wish there were a big fire on a hearth to toast my feet before, like Si does as he sleeps!"

"Ha, ha, ha!" laughed the boys as the young fellow stretched out on the board like Si.

A third boy then said, "Well, Si was named for two great men—his master, Dr. Josiah, and Dr. Josiah's uncle, Mr. Henson, who was an army officer." Other boys gave still other reasons for Si's greatness. However, the one thing upon which all were agreed was that Si could out-hoe, out-reap, out-husk, out-dance, out-everything every other boy on his master's plantation in Charles County, Maryland.

Si seemed to grow steadily in favor with his master and the older slaves as well as with the boys. One day he went to his master and reported that the overseer was stealing things at a certain time every day. His master sent him out to watch for the overseer. Just as the overseer came around for his booty, Si ran for his master. His master ran out and caught the overseer in the act of stealing and dismissed him at once.

Josiah, as his master called him, was then promoted to the position of superintendent of the farm, but without pay. He led the slaves. He hoed and plowed early and late. Men and women worked harder and far more cheerfully than usual. The crops were nearly doubled. Josiah often rose from his plank at midnight, hitched the mules to a loaded wagon and drove through mud and rain to the Georgetown or the Washington, D.C., market to sell the produce.

One day as he was selling at McKenny's bakery in Georgetown, he asked Mr. McKenny about a sermon which he had recently heard Mr. McKenny preach. After telling Mr. McKenny that that was the first sermon he had ever heard, he asked how men learned to preach.

Mr. McKenny told him a little about God and the Bible. He went further, saying, "My young man, you must be about nineteen or twenty years old now. You have a good mind. You must learn to preach to your people." This thought seemed to linger with Josiah as he made his way back home that evening hungry and tired.

His master, he learned, had been away at the tavern nearly all day. He ate his supper, called for his master's saddle horse, which he led to the tavern. As his master's body-servant, he alighted and went in. Just as he reached the door he saw his master cornered and a dozen men striking at him with their fists, chairs, crockery and whatever was at hand.

The moment Josiah's master saw him he shouted, "That's it, Josiah! Pitch in! Show me fair play!" Josiah pitched in. He knocked down and shoved and tripped up the fighters, sustaining many bruises on his own head and shoulders. Finally he was able to drag his master out and pack him into a wagon like a bag of corn and drive home. In the scuffle the overseer of Josiah's master's brother got a fall which he attributed to Josiah's roughness.

One week later Josiah's master sent him to a place a few miles away to mail some letters. He took a short cut through a lane which was bounded on either side by a high rail fence and shut in at each end by a large gate. As he passed through the line, he saw the overseer who had fallen that night and three slaves in an adjoining field. On his return, the overseer was seated on the fence. Just as Josiah approached, the overseer jumped from the fence. Two of the slaves sprang from the bushes in front of Josiah and the other slave leaped over the fence behind him. After listening to several commands to light at once, Josiah slipped off his horse. Orders were given him to remove his shirt, but he shook his head. Just then the men struck at him so violently that his horse broke away and ran home. Josiah, in warding off the blow, got into a corner. The overseer ordered the slaves to seize him, but they, knowing Josiah's reputation, hesitated to run upon him. The two slaves that finally ventured upon Josiah were so completely knocked out that the overseer began to fight like a madman. As he struck at Josiah with a piece of fence rail, Josiah lifted his arms to ward off the blow. The bones in Josiah's arms and shoulders cracked like pipe-stems, and he fell headlong to the ground.

When Josiah finally made his way home, his master, already anxious because of the return of the riderless horse, examined him and went in search of the overseer, whom he gave a severe flogging.

With the belief so well fixed that a slave would get well anyhow, no medical aid was provided for Josiah except what came at the hands of his master's sister,

Miss Patty. Miss Patty flinched at no responsibility, from wrenching out teeth to setting bones. She splinted Josiah's arms and bound up his back as well as she could.

Five months later, Josiah began to plow, to take up his duties as superintendent, and to make his usual trips to the markets. In about a year, although he was never able after that eventful day to raise his hands to his head, he married a rather efficient, pious girl who, as the years rolled on, bore him twelve children.

Josiah kept the slaves cheerful and busy. He furnished his master with abundance of money, which his master used freely on an eighteen-year-old girl whom he soon married.

The young mistress, in her attempt to save everything, failed to provide her younger brother, then living with her, with enough to eat. The boy went to Josiah with tears in his eyes and asked for food. Josiah shared his own provisions with him. However, in spite of the young mistress's frugality, her husband's good times involved him in debt and in lawsuits with his brother-in-law and others, and finally in ruin. He went to Josiah's cabin one cold night in January. As he sat by the fire warming himself, he began to groan and wring his hands.

"Sick, master?" said Josiah. He kept on groaning. "Can't I help you any way, master?" continued Josiah.

Finally pulling himself together, he said, "Oh, Josiah! I'm ruined, ruined, ruined!"

"How, master?" asked Josiah in excitement.

The master replied, "The courts have ruled against me, and in less than two weeks every slave I have will be put up and sold. There is only one way I can save anything. You can help me. Won't you, Josiah?"

"Yes," replied Josiah.

His master then said, "I want you to run away, Josiah, to my brother in Kentucky, and take all of my slaves with you." Josiah hesitated, saying that he did not know how to get to Kentucky. His master prevailed upon him until he promised to leave the following night for Kentucky.

The next morning Josiah set about making preparations for his journey. When evening came on he counted all of the slaves—eighteen in number, besides himself, his two children and his wife. He loaded a one-horse wagon with oats, meal, bacon and children, and set out about eleven o'clock for Kentucky, nearly a thousand miles away. The men trudged all the way in the cold. Occasionally the women rested by getting a ride on the wagon. After about two months and a half of wonderful experiences on the road, Josiah and the other slaves reached Davis County, Kentucky.

In that county Josiah's master's brother owned a large plantation and about one hundred slaves. Josiah became superintendent of that plantation after several months' stay there. He made himself about as content as he could under the circumstances. He occasionally attended preaching services and camp meetings. At the end of his three years' stay in Kentucky, a Quarterly Conference of the Methodist Episcopal Church admitted him as a minister. About this time Josiah's master sent an agent to Kentucky to sell all his slaves except Josiah and his family, who were to return to Maryland.

Directed by a Methodist minister, Josiah preached his way back through Ohio to Maryland, arriving with two hundred and seventy-five dollars, a horse and his first suit of clothes. His master greeted him, commented upon his fine clothes and sent him out to feed his horse. Josiah put his horse in the stable and went to the kitchen, where he was to sleep. He could not sleep for planning how to get his master to accept money for his freedom. His master was not easily persuaded. Nevertheless, he accepted three hundred and fifty dollars in cash as part payment for Josiah's freedom. Josiah set out again for Kentucky. Days passed before he was again back in his Kentucky cabin with his family. He became angry as soon as he heard how much more he had to pay before he could be free, and yet he went about his work as usual.

A year passed. One day Josiah's master told him that his son Amos was going to New Orleans with a flat-boat load of beef cattle, pigs, poultry, corn and whiskey. He said further that Josiah was to go with his son. Josiah's countenance fell. He said he feared he would never return. When he was ready to go, his wife and children walked to the landing with him, where he bade them good-bye.

Young master Amos, Josiah and three other men were the only persons on the boat. Each one except Josiah took his turn at the helm, usually under the direction of the captain. Josiah took three turns to each of the other men's one. He managed the boat so well that when the captain was struck totally blind on the trip, all depended upon him for reaching New Orleans in safety. However, he did not know the river well enough to travel by night; therefore the boat had to lay by when night came on.

One dark, stormy night, when they were within a few days' sail of New Orleans, Josiah sat knitting his brow and beating his breast in apparently hopeless despair. Suddenly he rose, saying, "I will kill the four men on the boat, take all the money, scuttle the boat and escape to the North." He walked alone on deck, while the other men were all asleep. Finally he went down, got an ax, and entered his young master's cabin where he lay fast asleep. Josiah raised the ax and was about to strike, but hesitated, saying, "What, commit murder, and I a Christian?" His arm dropped, the ax fell to the floor. Then he said to himself, "Ah, I am glad the thought took hold of me. Evil deeds cannot be hidden. 'Murder will out.' I must not lose all the fruits of my effort at improving myself. I must not lose my character." He shrank back and fell upon his knees.

Soon after they arrived in New Orleans, the cargo was all sold and the men were discharged. Josiah was to be sold the next day and Master Amos was to take passage back on a steamboat at six o'clock that evening.

Josiah could not sleep that night. Just a short while before daylight, Master Amos called him, saying, "My stomach is out of order." Josiah arose and went to him. His illness was so violent that Josiah saw at once that he had the river fever. By eight o'clock that morning he was helpless. He begged Josiah to stick to him until he reached home again. Josiah sold the flat-boat, placed his young master and the trunk containing the money for the cargo on the steamer and was off for Kentucky by twelve o'clock that day. As he sat by his master, bathing his fevered head, he could not help feeling that God had opened the way for his return to his family in Kentucky.

During the days that Josiah was preaching his way through Ohio, he had heard much about fugitive slaves. He had also met several men who were engaged in assisting fugitives to escape. All of this now came back to him very vividly.

He thought and thought, and then spoke to his wife about running away to the North. Struck with fear, she attempted to show him the dangers in their way. After pleading with her for several days, he told her one night that he was going to take the children and go. She, too, then agreed to go. Josiah wondered now how he could carry his younger children—one of whom was three years and the other only two. He placed them in a tow-sack which his wife had made, lifted it gently across his shoulder and practiced carrying them on his back. This he did for several nights.

Finally the evening in September agreed upon for their start came around. Everything was ready for the venture with one exception—Josiah had not obtained his master's permission to let little Tom, the eldest child, come home to see his mother. About sundown, he went up to the great house to report his work. After talking with his master for a time he started off as usual. Suddenly he turned carelessly back, saying, "Oh, Master Amos, I almost forgot. Tom's mother wishes to know if you will let him come down a few days; she would like to mend his clothes and fix him up a little."

"Yes, boy, yes, he can go," said Master Amos.

"Thank you, Master Amos, good night," said Josiah.

"Good night, Josiah," said he.

"The Lord bless you, Master Amos," added Josiah, as he and Tom struck a trot for home. Everybody at home was ready to start. The babies were even sitting in the sack. Soon they were all at the ferry. About nine o'clock on that moonless night, Josiah and his family were set across the river in a little skiff rowed by a fellow slave. They walked and walked until they were within two days of reaching Cincinnati, when their food gave out and they were nearly exhausted. Josiah ventured out to beg something for his children to eat. Finally a good woman filled a plate with salty venison and bread and gave it to him, saying, "God bless you."

The children ate and then cried for water. Josiah went in search of water and found a little. Seeing that his old hat leaked too badly to hold water, he pulled off both his shoes, rinsed them out and filled them with water, which he took to his thirsty children, who drank and drank until both shoes were drained.

Refreshed with food and water, they arose and continued their journey. After several weeks' travel they reached Sandusky, Ohio, where they secured passage to Buffalo, New York, with a Scotch captain. The Scotch captain, on reaching the end of his trip, paid their passage money on the ferry-boat across to Canada and gave Josiah one dollar besides. On the twenty-eighth of October, 1830, they arrived in Canada.

Josiah Henson began to work for a man with whom he remained three years. This man gave Tom,

Henson's twelve-year-old son, two quarters' schooling. Tom soon learned to read well, and he read a great deal to his father from the Bible on Sunday mornings when his father was to preach.

One Sunday morning Henson asked Tom to read. Tom turned to the One-hundred-and-third Psalm and read: "Bless the Lord, O my soul: and all that is within me, bless His holy name."

When he had finished, he turned to his father and said, "Father, who was David? He writes prettily, doesn't he?" And then Tom asked again, "Father, who was David?"

Henson said he was utterly unable to answer Tom's question, for he had never before heard of David, but he tried to conceal his embarrassment by saying, "David was a man of God, my son."

"I suppose so," said Tom, "but I want to know something more about him. Where did he live? What did he do?"

Finally Henson said frankly, "I do not know, Tom,"

Tom exclaimed, "Why, Father, can't you read?"

"I cannot," said Henson.

"Why not?" said Tom.

"Because I never had an opportunity to learn, nor anybody to teach me," replied Henson.

"Well, you can learn now, Father," said Tom.

"No, my son," answered Henson. "I am too old and have not time enough. I must work all day or you would not have enough to eat."

Tom said, "Then you might do it at night."

Henson thought a moment and, looking at his bright-eyed boy, said, "But still there's no-body to teach me. I can't afford to pay anybody for it, and of course, no one can do it for nothing."

Tom approached his father, saying, "Why Father, I'll teach you; and then you'll know so much more you can talk better and preach better." After wrestling with the matter a short time, Henson agreed that Tom was right. They began and continued through the winter to study together every evening by the light of a pine-knot or some hickory bark, until the coming of spring, when Henson had learned to read a little.

Now, at the age of fifty years, he was having some very new experiences. In line with his thought of establishing a school to help his people, he went to a Boston friend for aid, who in turn went to England and raised $15,000 for the school. With this money two hundred acres of land were bought at Dawn, Canada, on which, covered as it was with black walnut timber, a schoolhouse was built and opened to the public. Later a saw mill was built on this tract of land and set to running. The school and the sawmill prospered for a while, but soon both were in need of funds.

Henson had four black walnut boards so highly polished that they shone like mirrors. These he took to London, England, and exhibited at the World's Industrial Exhibition. For this exhibit he was awarded a bronze medal and a life-size picture of the Queen and royal family.

This was neither Henson's first nor his last trip to that country. After some years of trouble and sorrow and loss, he returned to England, just after the news had gone abroad that he was the original "Uncle Tom" of Harriet Beecher Stowe's "Uncle Tom's Cabin". This time many honors were heaped upon him. He even visited Windsor Castle and was presented to Queen Victoria, who presented him with a photograph of herself on an easel frame of gold.

On his return to the United States in 1878, he was received at the White House in Washington, D.C., by President Hayes. Before returning to Canada to spend the last three years of his life, he visited the old home place in Charles County, Maryland, where his former mistress, for whom he had worked fifty years before, and who was now poor and decrepit, wept for joy at the sight of him.

Sojourner Truth

The Suffragist
1800-1883

Among Isabella's earliest recollections was a picture of her father and mother sitting night after night in their damp cellar, lighted by a blazing pine-knot, talking over their experiences of bygone days. Occasionally they would refer to one snowy morning when an old-fashioned sleigh drove up to their door and took away their unsuspecting little boy, Michael, and their little girl, Nancy, locked in the sleigh-box.

Whenever this story was mentioned, Isabella seemed to fall into a deep study. However, she was left to remain in Ulster County, New York, her birthplace, until her mother and father died. She was then sold to a man whose wife scolded and frowned at her creeping gait, her dull understanding and slovenly ways. In spite of his wife's impatience, the man insisted that Isabella could do as much work as half a dozen common people and do it well.

Isabella, therefore, fond of trying to please her new master, often worked several nights in succession, taking only short naps as she sat in her chair. Some nights, fearing that if she sat down she would sleep too long, she took only cat-naps while she rested against the kitchen wall.

One morning the potatoes which Isabella had cooked for breakfast seemed unusually dingy and dirty. "Look!" said Isabella's mistress to her husband, "a fine specimen of Bell's work! It is the way all her work is done!" Isabella's master scolded her and bade her be more careful in the future. The two white servant-girls in the family also abused Isabella for preparing such food.

Isabella moped around apparently wondering why the potatoes looked so dingy and dirty. As she stood wondering how to avoid this the next time, Gertrude, her mistress's little daughter, stole quietly up behind her. Said she, catching Isabella by the arm, "Bell, if you will wake me early tomorrow morning, I will get up and attend to your potatoes while you go out to milk the cows. Then Father and Mother and all of them will not be scolding you." Isabella bowed, thanked her and promised to wake her early; then off Gertrude ran.

The next morning, just as the potatoes began to boil and milking time came, little Gertrude walked into the kitchen and seated herself in the Corner by the fire. She opened her little sewing basket and busied herself with making something for her doll. As she sat there, one of the maids came in with the broom in her hand and ordered her out, but Gertrude refused to go. The maid began to sweep hurriedly. When she reached the fireplace, she pretended to be in such a hurry, she caught up a handful of ashes and quickly dashed them into the potatoes. Gertrude ran out of the kitchen, saying, "Oh, Poppee! oh, Poppee! the girl has been putting ashes into Bell's potatoes! I saw her do it! Look at those that fell on the outside of the kettle!" She ran about the house and yard telling her story to everyone. Her father listened to her story, called the maid in and, brandishing his fist at her, gave her orders to let Bell alone.

For many years, Isabella tried harder each year to please her master. Even after she had married and become the mother of five children, she obeyed him to such an extent that she would not steal even a crust of bread for her hungry children. When her household duties were done, she went to the field to work. After placing her baby child in a basket, she tied a rope to each handle and suspended the basket to the branches of a tree. She then set one of the larger children to swing the basket "in order to make the baby happy and keep the snakes away," she said.

Isabella's master promised that if she would continue to be faithful he would set her free one year before all the slaves in New York State were to be free. As the time drew near, her master claimed that because of her sore hand that year, she had been of less value and would therefore have to remain longer. However, Isabella decided to remain only until she had spun all his wool.

One fine morning, a little before daybreak, she stepped away from the rear of her master's house with her baby boy on one arm and her clothes and provisions tied in a cotton handkerchief on the other. Fortunately, she landed in the home of a man who made no practice of buying and selling people. Nevertheless, he gave Isabella's master, who came in search of her, twenty-five dollars for her freedom.

Just before Isabella left her master, he had sold her five-year-old boy to a man who was on his way to England. The man, finding the boy too small for his services, sent him back to his brother, who in turn sold the boy to his brother-in-law in another state. When Isabella heard that her boy had been sold and sent away, she started out to find the guilty party and, if possible, to make him return her boy.

She went to her former mistress and others concerned in the sale, saying, "I'll have my child again." Finally she went to her former master, who told her to go to the Quakers and they would assist her. Straightway she went to the home of a Quaker family. They welcomed her and placed her in a room where there was a high, clean, white bed. In all of her twenty-seven years she had never slept in a bed. She sat for a long time looking at the bed and getting ready to crawl under it. However, she finally crawled gently up into the bed and soon fell asleep. The next morning, her Quaker friends took her nearly to town and gave her directions for reaching the court-house, where she made complaint to the grand jury.

On reaching the court-house, she entered. Thinking that the first fine-looking man she saw was the grand jury, she began to complain to him about her boy. He listened for a few moments and then told her that there was no grand jury there; she must go upstairs. When she had made her way upstairs through the crowd, she again went to the grandest-looking man she saw. Immediately she began to tell him that she came to make her complaint to the grand jury. Greatly amused, he asked what her complaint was. As soon as she began in her impressive way to tell her story, he said, pointing to a certain door. "This is no place to enter a complaint—go in there."

She went in, and finding the grand jurors sitting, began to tell her story. One of the jurors asked if she could swear that was her boy.

"Yes", she answered, "I swear it's my son."

"Stop, stop!" said the lawyer, "you must swear by this Bible." Taking the Bible, she placed it to her lips and began to swear it was her child. The clerks in the office burst into an uproar of laughter. None of this seemed to disturb Isabella. After understanding that she was simply to make a pledge of her truthfulness with her hand upon the Bible, she did so and hurried away. With a piece of paper, called a writ, in her hand for the arrest of the man who had sent her boy away, she trotted to the constable eight miles off. Although the constable by mistake served the writ on the wrong brother, it had its effect. The brother who had sold the boy went in hiding until he could slip away to get the boy.

The distance was great and travel in those days was slow. Autumn days came and went and then winter, and finally spring came before the man arrived with the boy. During all these months Isabella kept going about seeing this friend and that one, until she said she was afraid that she had worried all of her friends, even God himself, nearly to death.

The news finally reached her that her boy had come, but that he denied having any mother. When she reached the place where her boy Peter was, he cried aloud against this tall, dark, bony woman with a white turban on her head. He knelt down and begged with tears not to be taken from his kind master. When someone asked him about the bad scar on his forehead, he said, "Master's horse hove me there." And then someone else asked about the scar on his cheek. He said. "That was done by running against Master's carriage." As he answered both of these questions, he looked wistfully at his master, as much as to say, "If they are falsehoods, you bade me say them; may they be satisfactory to you, at least."

Kind words and candies at last quieted Peter and he said, looking at his mother. "Well, you do look like my mother used to look." They embraced each other and went their way.

After Isabella and Peter had been free one year they went to New York City to live. Peter was growing tall and rather nice-looking, in spite of his hard life. He often attracted attention by his winsome way; but tempted by the gay life of New York City, he was soon drawn into a circle of boys whose sole object was to have a good time. He began to conceal from his mother those things of which he thought she would not approve. For example, for two years he was known among his worthless companions as Peter Williams, without his mother's knowledge of his new name. However, a friend of Isabella's, much pleased with Peter's appearance and bright mind, said that Peter should have an education if anyone else should. Believing this, she paid ten dollars as tuition for him to enter a navigation school. Instead of attending school, Peter went irregularly, making some reasonable excuse each time to his teacher for not being able to attend school that day. Isabella and her friend, believing that Peter was doing well in school, secured for him a part-time job as coachman. Peter soon sold the livery and other things belonging to his employer.

He became involved in one difficulty after another, but each time Isabella managed to get him out. Each time she tried to reason with Peter. He would always confess, saying that he never intended to do wrong, but had been led along little by little until before he knew it, he was in serious trouble. At last, seeing no improvement in her son, Isabella made up her mind to let him go unassisted in his difficulties. Finally, he fell into the hands of the police, who sent for Mr. Peter Williams, a barber. Mr. Williams's interest was so aroused by the boy's having his name, that he paid the fine on Peter's promise to leave New York City on a vessel sailing within a week.

Mr. Williams seemed surprised to find that the boy had such a mother as Isabella. Isabella said that she was afraid lest her son would deceive Mr. Williams and be missing when the vessel sailed. However, Peter sailed; though for over a month Isabella lived in fear of seeing him emerge from some by-street in New York City. More than a year had passed when Isabella received the following letter:

My dear and beloved Mother:

I take this opportunity to write to you and inform you that I am well, and in hopes of finding you the same. I got on board the same unlucky ship "Done of Nantucket". I am sorry to say that I have been punished once severely by shoving my head in the fire for other folks. We have had bad luck, but in hopes of having better. We have about 230 on board, but in hopes, if we do have good luck, that my parents will receive me with thanks.

I would like to know how my sisters are. Do my cousins live in New York yet? Have you received my letter? If not, inquire of Mr. Peirce Whitings. I wish you would write me an answer as soon as possible. I am your only son, that is so far from home, in the wide, briny ocean. I have seen more of the world than I ever expected, and if I ever return home safe, I will tell you all my troubles and hardships. Mother, I hope you do not forget me, your dear and only son. I should like to know how Sophia and Betsy and Hannah are. I hope you all will forgive me for all that I have done.

Your son,
PETER VAN WAGNER.

Isabella's last annual letter from Peter said that if he did not do well, she need not expect him home in five years. During the five years of expectant waiting, Isabella joined Zion's Church, in Church Street, New York City, where she worshiped for some time. One Sunday morning, after services, a tall, well-dressed woman came up and made herself known to Isabella as her sister Sophia who had just moved to New York City. She also brought to meet Isabella her brother Michael, whom Isabella had never seen. The brother Michael told Isabella that her sister Nancy, who had been for many years a member of Zion Church, had just passed away. As he described his sister Nancy's features, her manner, her dress, and named her class leader, Isabella stood shaking as though she would fall to the floor. She caught hold of the back of a bench, exclaiming, "I knelt at the altar with her. I took the Lord's Supper with her. I shook hands with her! Was that my sister who was taken away one snowy morning in the sleigh? Are you my brother Michael who was taken away in the sleigh-box?" The three of them stood there mingling their tears each with the other.

While Isabella was a member of Zion Church she often visited the pavement meetings of a band of religious fanatics. These fanatics were in the habit of fasting every Friday and sometimes as long as two nights and three days, refusing even a cup of cold water. Isabella asked one of the leaders why he fasted. He said that fasting gave him great light on the things of God. "Well," said Isabella, "if fasting will give light inwardly and spiritually, I need it as much as anybody, and I'll fast too." She further said, "If such a good man as that needs to fast two nights and three days, then I certainly ought to fast more. I will fast three nights and three days."

She fasted three nights and three days, not drinking even so much as a drop of water. The fourth morning when she arose and tried to stand, she fell to the floor. Feeling very empty and light, she crawled to the pantry, but fearing, as she says, that she might now offend God by eating too much, she compelled herself to eat dry bread and drink water. Before she felt strong enough to walk she had eaten a six-penny loaf of bread. She says that she did get light, but it was all in her body and none in her mind.

During Isabella's first years in New York City, she was always trying to place a little money from time to time in the savings bank for the rainy day. Influenced by her fanatic friends, she drew her money from the savings bank and placed it in their common treasury, or kingdom, as they called it, not even asking about interest or taking account of what she had put in. In later years Isabella often said in her witty way, "The only thing I recovered from the wreck of that common kingdom was a few pieces of old furniture."

With all of her savings gone, she started anew, working early and late, to lay aside enough to buy a home for herself in her advanced age. If the people in the home where she worked gave her fifty cents to hire a poor man to clean away the snow, she arose early, performed the task herself and pocketed the money. She began to feel that she, too, was robbing the poor in her selfish grasping.

She talked much about this. It seemed to prey on her mind. Finally she decided to leave New York City and travel east and lecture. With the secret locked in her own bosom, she made ready for leaving by placing a few articles of clothing in a pillow-case. About an hour before starting out, she went to the woman at whose house she was staying and said, "My name is no longer Isabella, but 'Sojourner'. I am going east. The spirit calls me there, and I must go."

On the morning of June 1, 1843, Sojourner, now forty-three years old, set out from New York City with her pillow-case in one hand, a little basket of provisions in the other and two York shillings in her purse. As she crossed over to Brooklyn, she says she thought of Lot's wife, and, wishing to avoid her fate, was determined not to look back until New York City was far in the distance. When night came on she sought for a lodging place wherever she could find one.

It was her plan, as she explained, when she became weary of travel and needed rest, to stop at some home for a few days. The very first time she felt the need of rest badly, as she walked along the road, a man addressed her, asking if she were looking for work. "Sir," she said in her queenly way, "that's not the object of my travels, but if you need me I can help you out for a few days." She went in and worked so faithfully that the man offered her at the time of her departure what seemed to her a large sum of money. Refusing all except two or three York shillings which she considered sufficient to take her on her mission, she went her way.

After she had traveled far out on Long Island, one evening, in her search for a night's lodging, she met two Indians who took her for an acquaintance. They asked if she were alone. Not knowing anything at all about them, she replied, "No, not exactly," and kept going.

In her search for lodging places, Sojourner Truth occasionally went into dance-halls and hovels of the lowest kind. Nevertheless, she traveled on foot lecturing in many New York and Connecticut towns. Then led, as she claimed, by the spirit, she continued her journey to Northampton, Massachusetts.

One night, while she was living at Northampton, she attended a camp-meeting which was being held in the open air. Those attending the meeting slept in tents. A company of boys present said they were going to set fire to all the tents. Those in charge of the meeting sent for the sheriff to arrest the ring-leaders. Sojourner Truth rushed to hide in one corner of a tent. She said, "Shall I run away and hide from the devil? Me a servant of the Living God? Have I not faith enough to go out and quell that mob when I know it is written one shall chase a thousand and two put ten thousand to flight?" She walked out from her hiding-place, under the moonlight, to the top of a small rise of ground and began to sing:

It was early in the morning—it was early in the morning,
Just at the break of day—
When He rose—when He rose—when He rose—
And went to heaven on a cloud.

The boys with their sticks and clubs made a rush towards her and crowded around her. She stopped singing and after a few minutes asked in a gentle but firm tone, "Why do you come about me with clubs and sticks? I am not doing harm to any one."

Many of them said, "We are not going to hurt you, old woman. We came to hear you sing."

"Sing to us," another cried.

"Tell us your experience," said another.

182

"You stand and smoke so near me, I can't sing or talk," she answered. They immediately removed their cigarettes and cigars. At their suggestion and with their help, she climbed upon a wagon nearby and spoke and sang for nearly an hour. Upon asking the third time if they would go away and act like men, all yelled out, "Yes, yes!"

She traveled a great deal, holding many meetings for the sake of the freedom of her people. Imagine this big, bony, black woman, six feet tall, walking along the highway or riding along with a small clay pipe in her mouth from which rolled columns of smoke. One evening she was riding in the State of Iowa on a railroad train. A man sitting in a seat just behind her saw her smoking and said to her, "Do you believe in the Bible?"

"I do," she replied.

"Well, then," said he, "what can be more filthy than the breath of a smoker? Doesn't the Bible say no unclean thing shall enter the kingdom of heaven?"

"Yes, child," she answered, "but when I go to heaven I expect to leave my breath behind me."

Even before the Civil War, she held meetings in many states. At the close of a meeting in Ohio one evening, a man came up to her and said, "Old woman, do you think that your talk about slavery does any good? Do you suppose people care what you say? I don't care anymore for your talk than I do for the bite of a flea."

"Perhaps not," she answered, "but the Lord willing, I'll keep you a-scratching."

Once when she was out on a speaking tour she met a man who asked, "What business are you following now?"

She quickly replied, "Years ago when I lived in New York City my occupation was scouring brass door-knobs, but now I go about scouring copper-heads."

She could neither read nor write. She seemed to know, however, something about many of the big subjects of the day, such as "Suffrage", "Temperance" and "Abolition". She even attended the first big woman's suffrage convention, held in Ohio. This convention was held in a church. Sojourner Truth marched in like a queen and sat on the pulpit steps. In those days men thought women should not vote. The men and even the boys were laughing at the women and teasing them for holding such a meeting.

Old "Sojourner Truth" rose and walked out in front of the speakers' table. She took off her sun-bonnet and laid it at her feet. Many of the women said, "Don't let that old woman speak. She will do us harm."

But the presiding officer rapped on the table for order and "Sojourner Truth" began by saying, "Well, children, where there is so much racket there must be something out of kilter." She had something sharp to say in reply to every minister who had spoken. One minister had said that women should not vote because Eve had acted so badly. To him she said, "If the first woman God ever made was strong enough to turn the world upside down, all alone, these together [glancing around over all the women] ought to be able to turn it right side up again."

She took her seat in the midst of great applause. Many women rushed to her, shook her hand and said, "You have saved the day."

One day while Lincoln was President of the United States, Sojourner, old and bent, walked into the marble room of the Senate Chamber. It was an hour not soon to be forgotten. Senators rose and shook her hand. They asked her to speak. As she spoke, some sat with tears in their eyes. When she had finished they shook her hand again, gave her a purse and bade her good-bye. A Washington Sunday paper had a long article about Sojourner Truth's speaking to the United States Senators. This article said: "Sojourner Truth has had a marvelously strange life. The leaven of love must be working in the hearts of all people."

In her old age and suffering, Sojourner Truth was supported by a friend. The end came at Battle Creek, Michigan, November 26, 1883.

Crispus Attucks
1723-1770

Crispus Attucks was born many years ago, at some place, but nobody in the world seems to know just where. And no one seems to know anything at all about him, or about his people, except that he was a sailor. He received public notice just twice in his lifetime. The first time it was through an advertisement in a Boston newspaper, which came out on the second of October, 1750. The advertisement read:

Ran away from his master, William Brown of Framingham, on the 30th of September, last, a Molatto-Fellow, about twenty-seven years of age, named Crispus, 6 feet 2 inches high, short curl'd hair, his knees nearer together than common; had on a light color'd Bearskin Coat, plain brown Fustain Jacket, or brown all-wool one, new Buck skin Breeches, blue yarn stockings, and a checked woolen shirt.

Whoever shall take up said Runaway, and convey him to his above said Master, shall have ten pounds, Old Tenor Reward, and all necessary charges paid.

Boston, Oct. 2, 1750.

The name of Crispus Attucks appeared in the Boston papers just once more, and that was twenty years later, at the time of the Boston Massacre. In those days Crispus Attucks knew nothing about the United States, and nobody else did, for there were no United States. There were only the American colonies of Great Britain.

Because Great Britain knew that these colonies were angry with her, she sent several regiments of soldiers over to Boston, Massachusetts. These soldiers were to make the colonies obey England. Everyone in Boston seemed to be speaking against these British soldiers.

Finally a group of men led by Crispus Attucks began to pelt them with missiles and chunks of ice, and to dare them to fire their guns, but the British soldiers fired. Shells from their guns struck Crispus Attucks and three other men. Crispus Attucks and one of the men, by the name of Caldwell, fell dead. The other two were mortally wounded.

The whole city of Boston was in an uproar. Bells were ringing everywhere, and people were running here and there as if they were crazy. In the midst of all of this excitement, the bodies of Crispus Attucks and Caldwell were taken into Faneuil Hall. It is said that their faces were looked upon by the largest gathering of people ever assembled there. One of the men who fell was buried from his mother's home. Another was buried from his brother's home, but Attucks and Caldwell, being strangers in the city, were buried from Faneuil Hall.

The four hearses bearing the bodies of the dead men met in King Street. From there the funeral procession moved in columns six deep. There was an extended line of carriages containing the first citizens of Boston. The four bodies were buried in one grave, and over the grave was placed a stone with this inscription:

Long as in Freedom's cause the wise contend,
Dear to your Country shall your fame extend;
While to the world the lettered stone shall tell
Where Caldwell, Attucks, Gray and Maverick fell.

Crispus Attucks is sometimes called a madcap, because he led the Boston Massacre charge, which was the beginning of the Revolutionary War. He had apparently been around Boston for some years and had listened to the fiery speeches of some of the orators of that day.

A memorial shaft was later erected on Boston Common to the memory of these men, and a memorial tablet was placed on State Street in Boston.

CRISPUS ATTUCKS

Read at the Dedication of the Crispus Attucks Monument in Boston, November 14, 1888

*Where shall we seek for a hero, and where shall we
    find a story?*
*Our laurels are wreathed for conquest, our songs for
    completed glory.*
*But we honor a shrine unfinished, a column uncapped
    with pride,*
*If we sing the deed that was sown like seed when
    Crispus Attucks died.*

*Shall we take for a sign this Negro-slave with
    unfamiliar name—*
*With his poor companions nameless too, till their lives
    leaped forth in flame?*
Yea, surely, the verdict is not for us to render or deny;
*We can only interpret the symbol; God chose these
    men to die—*
*As teachers and types, that to humble lives may chief
    award be made;*

Crispus Attucks

That from lowly ones, and rejected stones, the
    temple's base is laid!

When the bullets leaped from the British guns, no
    chance decreed their aim:
Men see what the royal hirelings saw—a multitude
    and a flame;
But beyond the flame, a mystery; five dying men in
    the street,
While the streams of several races in the well of a
    nation meet!

O, blood of the people! changeless tide, through
    century, creed and race!
Still one as the sweet salt sea is one, though tempered
    by sun and place;
The same in the ocean currents, and the same in the
    sheltered seas;
Forever the fountain of common hopes and kindly
    sympathies;
Indian and Negro, Saxon and Celt, Teuton and Latin
    and Gaul—
Mere surface shadow and sunshine; while the
    sounding unifies all!
One love, one hope, one duty theirs! No matter the
    time or ken,
There never was separate heart-beat in all the races
    of men!

But alien is one—of class, not race—he has drawn the
    line for himself;
His roots drink life from inhuman soil, from garbage
    of pomp and pelf;
His heart beats not with the common beat, he has
    changed his life-stream's hue;
He deems his flesh to be finer flesh, he boasts that his
    blood is blue:
Patrician, aristocrat, tory—whatever his age or
    name,
To the people's rights and liberties, a traitor ever the
    same.
The natural crowd is a mob to him, their prayer a
    vulgar rhyme;
The freeman's speech is sedition, and the patriot's
    deed a crime.
Wherever the race, the law, the land—whatever the
    time, or throne,
The tory is always a traitor to every class but his own.

Thank God for a land where pride is clipped, where
    arrogance stalks apart;
Where law and song and loathing of wrong are words
    of the common heart;
Where the masses honor straightforward strength,
    and know, when veins are bled,

Crispus Attucks

That the bluest blood is putrid blood—that the
    people's blood is red!

And honor to Crispus Attucks, who was leader and
    voice that day;
The first to defy, and the first to die, with Maverick,
    Carr, and Gray.
Call it riot or revolution, his hand first clenched at the
    crown;
His feet were the first in perilous place to pull the
    king's flag down;
His breast was the first one rent apart that liberty's
    stream might flow;
For our freedom now and forever, his head was the
    first laid low.

                —John Boyle O'Reilly.

Paul Cuffé

The Sailor
1759-1817

The Cuffé home at Westport, Massachusetts, was always ringing with laughter and merriment. Somebody in that family of four sturdy boys, six girls, mother and father, was ever ready with a snappy joke, or a ghostly yarn which sometimes made even the old folks afraid to go to bed.

One night the family was seated around the hearth. Father Cuffé began to tell what he called a true story about his native country. He rose and pictured a great boa-constrictor gliding into his African home and swallowing a little boy. As he represented the great open mouth of that huge snake with the boy slipping down its throat, one of the girls jumped and looked behind her. The boys laughed very heartily and pointed their fingers at her, saying, "You thought that boa-constrictor had you!" Mrs. Cuffé, who was of Indian descent, attracted the family's attention just at that point by springing forth suddenly with a war-whoop and dance.

As soon as this came to an end, Paul Cuffé, the youngest of the boys, began telling one of his whale stories. He, too, arose and described his boat as it rocked to and fro on a stormy sea. He pictured his men tugging at a great whale, which suddenly pulled one of them overboard. Just then one of Paul's brothers gave a quick jerk on Paul's coat-tail. Paul leaped forward, looked back and landed flat on the floor. His sisters and brothers laughed and laughed until some of them said their sides ached.

Such evenings in the Cuffé farmhouse at Westport were common until Father Cuffé died. Paul was then fourteen years old. For two years, he and his brothers worked their poor farm of one hundred acres and thus supported their mother and sisters as best they could.

Every day spent in the field seemed harder and harder to Paul. He had made up his mind, he said, to try his fortune on the sea, but dreaded to tell his mother. One morning he lingered around until there was no one in the house but him and his mother. "Mother," he said, "I am big for my age, and if I can get a job on a schooner, I can earn a man's wages. I can make it on the sea better than on the land."

His mother held up both hands, saying, "Paul, my dear boy, can't you find something else to do? Sailors are such rough men. They drink, they swear, they are reckless."

"Mother," said he, "I have always longed to be a sailor. Give me your consent." For several days there was no laughter in the Cuffé home. Paul's mother said she feared he would be swallowed up by the angry waves or by a whale.

During these days, Paul was as busy as he could be trying to get a job on a schooner. Finally, he succeeded in hiring out as a common hand on a vessel leaving on a whaling expedition for the Bay of Mexico. His mother was sure now that Paul would never return alive, so she gave him a small Bible and her blessing. He kissed her good bye, pressed her hand and assured her that he would remain a good boy.

By nine o'clock the next morning, everything was in readiness for the start. The wind was favorable. The skipper was on board. Every sailor was busy making sail or getting up the heavy anchor. At length the schooner glided away from the shore.

For a time, Paul and the rest of the hands were busy coiling lines, stowing away odds and ends and making the vessel comfortable. As soon as Paul had a few spare moments he filled a small keg with fresh water and put several dozen ship-biscuits into a box, around which he wrapped an old oilskin jacket. One of the boys on board laughed at him and said in loud tones, "Are you afraid of being lost in a fog? Boy, your mamma's apron strings are many miles away. You should have been tied to them instead of being on a boat."

One of Paul's friends started to answer back, but Paul said, "Let him alone. It will make him feel worse not to be noticed at all."

The schooner tugged away until the end of the journey was finally reached. The trip was exciting to say the least; and their return trip was equally exciting. They had been gone for some weeks. In those days vessels traveled only about seven knots an hour. Paul had just a few hours at home with his mother before setting out on a trip to the West Indies. At the end of this trip, he seemed to feel that he was a full-fledged sailor. It had taken him only two weeks to get sufficient experience in navigation to command a vessel. He went out on a third voyage, but the Revolutionary War broke out. His ship was run down and captured by a British ship, and he was held as a prisoner for three months.

After his release, Cuffé had to give up the sea for two years. He visited the Island of Cuttyhunk, near New Bedford, where he was born. Then he returned to his home at Westport, worked on the farm and gave much of his time to the betterment of his people. He was not yet twenty years old, but he and his brother drew up a petition and presented it to the Massachusetts Legislature. This petition asked that all free people of Massachusetts be given the full rights of citizens. The Massachusetts Legislature carefully considered this respectful petition. Soon afterward it passed an act granting to all free people, irrespective of color, the full privileges of citizens.

Cuffé was busy these two years and yet his old longing for business and for the sea, he said, kept stealing over him. He laid before his brother, David, a plan for trading with the people of Connecticut. His brother agreed to the plan. They built an open boat and put out to sea, but his brother's fears so increased that he resolved to turn back. Paul finally submitted and returned home.

He worked a while for more materials and again put out to sea, but soon lost all he had. He went home and set himself to the task of making a boat from keel to gunwale. It was without a deck, but Paul had been on whaling expeditions and was thereby skilled in its management. He launched his boat into the ocean. As he was steering for Cuttyhunk, one of the Elizabeth Islands, to consult his brother about future plans, he was discovered by pirates, who chased his vessel, ran it down and captured both it and him.

He went home again and applied to his brother David for materials to build another boat. When the boat was finished, through his credit (on his respectability), he purchased a cargo and set out for Nantucket. On this voyage, he was again chased by pirates, but he escaped them as night came on. However, his boat struck upon a rock and was so injured that he had to return home for repairs. As soon as the repairs were made, he set out again for Nantucket and arrived in safety. On his return trip, however, he fell into the hands of pirates and was robbed of all he had except his boat. He made his way home, secured a small cargo and again directed his course towards Nantucket, where he sold his cargo to advantage.

On his return to his home this time, he secured a small covered boat of about twelve tons, hired someone to assist him, and made advantageous voyages to different parts of Connecticut.

He now became attached to a young woman—a descendant of his mother's tribe—whom he married. After his marriage he worked on a farm for a short while, then removed his family to a small house on the Westport River. He procured a boat of eighteen tons in which he sailed to the banks of St. George, obtained a valuable cargo of codfish and landed at home safely.

Cuffé soon entered partnership with his brother-in-law and built a vessel of twenty-five tons, in which they made voyages to Newfoundland and Belle Isle, securing profits enough to build a vessel of forty-two tons.

After the death of Cuffé's father he learned to read, write and do some arithmetic and yet he often said, "I would have made fewer mistakes and a great deal more money had I been an educated man." He called the people of his neighborhood together and spoke to them on the need of a schoolhouse and a teacher for their children. No two of the parents seemed to agree on anything. They talked and discussed and separated, each going to his own home. Paul Cuffé took the matter into his own hands, erected a schoolhouse on his own land and opened it to the public.

With this task completed, he set out to the Straits of Belle Isle on a whaling expedition, with two boats and ten men. Although he was ill prepared for the business, he and his crew killed six whales; two of which died at Paul's own hands. In due season he returned home heavily laden with bone and oil.

After selling his cargo, he bought iron and other materials, built a schooner of sixty-nine tons and launched it, in 1795, under the name of "The Ranger". He sold his two boats and placed on board "The Ranger", which was manned by a black crew, a cargo valued at two thousand dollars, and sailed for Norfolk, Virginia. This trip and similar ones brought him handsome returns.

With some of this money he bought a farm and placed it under the management of his brother-in-law. He also took one-half share in building and fitting out a large vessel, and three-fourths' share in building and fitting out still a larger one. One of these vessels, of one hundred and sixty-two tons burden, was commanded by Paul Cuffé's nephew. The other one, "The Alpha" by name, of two hundred and sixty-eight tons, was commanded by Paul Cuffé himself, with seven other Negroes making up the crew.

In 1811, Paul Cuffé and his crew, in command of "The Alpha" sailed for Sierra Leone, Africa. After many days of travel and stormy sea, they arrived in Sierra Leone. Cuffé, attended by several natives, made his way to the governor's office, where he remained for a long conversation and visit with the Governor.

Following this, he entered into many of the natives' experiences. He put on armor and went elephant-hunting with them. Once he joined a party on a leopard hunt. One of the party said in his native tongue, "These leopards go about in pairs, and sometimes raid farms and carry off young children and chickens after dark. They step rather softly, steal upon one and attack him in the back." When the party reached a certain spot, every one stopped. Some of them proceeded to drive down two posts. Others loaded a long-range gun heavily and fastened it to these posts with the butt end resting on the posts and the muzzle about two feet from them. Then they placed a big piece of meat around the muzzle of the gun and drew a strong string round one of the posts connecting the meat to the trigger. All was in readiness now for Mr. Leopard; and so the party left the spot. After a long wait a leopard came walking softly by and sniffing around. He walked up to the meat to take a bite. "Pow," went the rifle. The leopard fell dead. Paul Cuffé and his party came out from their hiding place, and stood around looking at the beast.

Cuffé seemed very busy, even on such trips, studying the needs of natives and planning how the people in London might help them. One morning a monkey party came to take him along. He could not resist the invitation. Everyone in the party had a sword or a stick. Several monkeys were caught that day and brought in tied hand and foot and hung on poles. The suckling ones were carried clinging underneath their mothers' bodies. Cuffé continued to study the natives and finally recommended to the Governor that they form "The Friendly Society of Sierra Leone" as a help to the people.

After this was done, he went to England on two trips. Then he returned to the United States in order to get teachers to take back with him, but the War of 1812 broke out, and his plans were delayed. For several years he had to remain in the United States. All this time, however, he was arranging to take teachers to Sierra Leone.

Toward the end of the year 1815, he sailed with thirty-eight teachers for Sierra Leone. For fifty-five days they were tossed and driven on the ocean. Even African soil, they said, was a welcome sight to them.

They finally reached their destination safely. Cuffé bore the entire expense of the trip.

He remained in Sierra Leone two months, during which time he wrote a very touching letter to the natives. It is said that his departure from them was like that of a father taking leave of his children.

Cuffé returned to his own country, where he became ill early in 1817. From then until the day of his death, on the seventh of the following September, he was busy writing letters and making friends for the natives of Sierra Leone. Someone has said that he devoted even the thoughts of his dying pillow to the interests of the African people.

Paul Cuffé

Paul Cuffé was born in 1759 on the island of Cuttyhunk, near New Bedford, Massachusetts. There were four sons and six daughters of John Cuffé who had been stolen from Africa, and Ruth, a woman of Indian extraction. Paul, the youngest son, lacked the advantage of an early education, but he supplied the deficiency by his personal efforts and learned not only to read and write with facility, but made such proficiency in the art of navigation as to become a skillful seaman and the instructor of both whites and blacks in the same art.

His father, who had obtained his freedom and bought a farm of one hundred acres, died when Paul was about fourteen. When he was sixteen, Paul began the life of a sailor. On his third voyage he was captured by a British brig and was for three months a prisoner of war. On his release he planned to go into business on his own account. With the aid of an elder brother, David Cuffé, an open boat was built in which they went to sea; but this brother on the first intimation of danger gave up the venture and Paul was forced to undertake the work single-handed and alone, which was a sore disappointment. On his second attempt he lost all he had.

Before the close of the Revolutionary War, Paul refused to pay a personal tax, on the ground that free colored people did not enjoy the rights and privileges of citizenship. After considerable delay, and an appeal to the courts, he paid the tax under protest. He then petitioned to the legislature which finally agreed to his contention. His efforts are the first of which there is any record of a citizen of African descent making a successful appeal in behalf of his civil rights. On reaching the age of twenty-five he married a woman of the same tribe as his mother, and for a while gave up life on the ocean wave; but the growth of his family led him back to his fond pursuit on the briny deep. As he was unable to purchase a boat, with the aid of his brother he built one from keel to gunwale and launched into the enterprise.

While on the way to a nearby island to consult his brother whom he had induced once more to venture forth with him, he was overtaken by pirates who robbed him of all he possessed. Again Paul returned home disappointed, though not discouraged. Once more he applied for assistance to his brother David and another boat was built. After securing a cargo, he met again with pirates, but he eluded them though he was compelled to return and repair his boat. These having been made, he began a successful career along the coast as far north as Newfoundland, to the south as far as Savannah and as distant as Gottenburg.

In carrying on this business, starting in the small way indicated, he owned at different times besides smaller boats, "The Ranger," a schooner of sixty or seventy tons, a half interest in a brig of 162 tons, the brig "Traveller," of 109 tons, the ship "Alpha," of 268 tons and three-fourths interest in a larger vessel.

A few noble incidents may illustrate his resourcefulness, difficulties and success over all obstacles. When engaged in the whaling business he was found with less than the customary outfit for effectually carrying on this work. The practice in such cases was for the other ships to loan the number of men needed. They denied this at first to Cuffé, but fair play prevailed and they gave him what was customary, with the result that of the seven whales captured, Paul's men secured five, and two of them fell by his own hand!

In 1795 he took a cargo to Norfolk, Virginia, and learning that corn could be bought at a decided advantage, he made a trip to the Nanticoke River, on the eastern shore of Maryland. Here his appearance as a black man commanding his own boat and with a crew of seven men all of his own complexion, alarmed the whites, who seemed to dread his presence there as the signal for a revolt on the part of their slaves. They opposed his landing, but the examination of his papers removed all doubts as to the regularity of his business, while his quiet dignity secured the respect of the leading white citizens. He had no difficulty after this in taking a cargo of three thousand bushels of corn, from which he realized a profit of $1000. On a second voyage he was equally successful.

Although without the privilege of attending a school when a boy, he endeavored to have his friends and neighbors open and maintain one for the colored and Indian children of the vicinity. Failing to secure their active cooperation, he built in 1797 a schoolhouse without their aid.

Because of his independent means and his skill as a mariner, he visited with little or no difficulty most of the larger cities of the country, held frequent conferences with the representative men of his race, and recommended the formation of societies for their mutual relief and physical betterment. Such societies he formed in Philadelphia and New York, and then having made ample preparation he sailed in 1811 for Africa in his brig "The Traveller," reaching Sierra Leone on the West Coast after a voyage of about two months.

Here he organized the Friendly Society of Sierra Leone and then went to Liverpool. Even here one of his characteristic traits manifested itself in taking with him to England for education a native of Sierra Leone.

While in England, Cuffé visited London twice and consulted such friends of the Negro as Granville Sharp, Thomas Clarkson and William Wilberforce! These men were all interested in a proposition to promote the settlement on the West Coast of Africa of the free people of color in America, many of whom had come into the domains of Great Britain as an outcome of the Revolutionary War. This opinion was at this period the prevailing sentiment of England respecting what was best for the Negro. Sir J.J. Crooks, a former governor of Sierra Leone, in alluding to its origin, says: "There is no doubt that the influence of their opinion was felt in America and that it led to emigration thence to Africa before Liberia was settled. Paul Cuffé, a man of color...who was much interested in the promotion of the civil and religious liberty of his colored brethren in their native land, had been familiar with the ideas of these philanthropists, as well as with the movement in the same direction in England."

This explains Cuffé's visit to England and to Africa—a daring venture in those perilous days—and the formation of the Friendly Societies in Africa and in his own country, the United States.

When his special mission to England was concluded, he took out a cargo from Liverpool for Sierra Leone, after which he returned to America.

Before he made his next move, Cuffé consulted with the British Government in London and President Madison at Washington. But the strained relations between the two nations, as well as the financial condition of the United States at the time, made governmental cooperation impracticable if not impossible.

In 1815 he carried out the ideas long in his mind. In this year he sailed from Boston for Sierra Leone with thirty-eight free Negroes as settlers on the Black Continent. Only eight of these could pay their own expenses, but Cuffé, nevertheless, took out the entire party, landed them safe on the soil of their forefathers after a journey of fifty-five days and paid the expense for the outfit, transportation and maintenance of the remaining thirty, amounting to no less than twenty-five thousand dollars ($25,000), out of his own pocket. The colonists were cordially welcomed by the people of Sierra Leone, and each family received from thirty to forty acres from the Crown Government. He remained with the settlers two months and then returned home with the purpose of taking out another colony. Before, however, he could do so, and while preparations were being made for the second colony, he was taken ill. After a protracted illness he died September 7, 1817, in the fifty-ninth year of his age. At the time of his death he had no less than two thousand names of intending emigrants on his list awaiting transportation to Africa.

As to his personal characteristics: Paul Cuffé was "tall, well-formed and athletic, his deportment conciliating yet dignified and prepossessing. He was a member of the Society of Friends (Quakers) and became a minister among them ... He believed it to be his duty to sacrifice private interest, rather than engage in any enterprise, however lawful...or however profitable, that had the slightest tendency to injure his fellow man. He would not deal in intoxicating liquors or in slaves."

Alexander Crummell

Minister and Missionary
1819-1898

One moonlight night about eighty-four years ago, a stage-coach rattled along from Hanover, New Hampshire, towards Albany, New York. Away up on the top of this stage-coach, sat two fast friends, Alexander Crummell and Henry Highland Garnet, and twelve other Negro boys. Apparently not even the rattle of the stage coach wheels, or the jingle of the traces, or the hoot of an owl far off in the woods, disturbed their thoughts. It is true, they had been riding all day and had been under excitement for two days before they left the little town of Canaan near Hanover, but they neither slept nor stirred.

A thoughtless gang of Canaan boys had yoked about one hundred and ninety oxen together and driven them up to the little schoolhouse. Here and there, one ox tried to go one way while his mate tried to go the other way, but several yoke of them did team-work. They later bowed their necks and chased off through the woods, with the boys swinging to the lines and bumping against stumps and logs and trees.

Finally, with the assistance of big boys, these unruly animals were brought back to the schoolhouse, to which the oxen were hitched.

At the crack of many long whips and the sound of loud calls, "Get up there, now! Pull steady," the oxen gave a mighty pull, and the sides of the little schoolhouse began to crack.

After two days of being pulled and pushed about, the little schoolhouse tottered into the swamp. The village boys, who had declared they would not let the Negro boys remain there and go to school, gave a cheer and a whoop. Still more excitement followed until Crummell and his friends took the stage-coach enroute for their homes.

This bitter experience seemed only to sharpen Crummell's desire for an education. In a few months, he was off again to a school some distance from New York City—his birthplace and home. After his graduation from that school, a ceremony was performed and he became a priest in the Episcopal Church.

He worked at home a while, and then crossed the Atlantic Ocean and preached throughout England. While he was there, he entered a great university known as Cambridge University, from which he was graduated at the age of thirty-four.

Crummell often spoke of wishing to return to the United States to see his family and friends, but because of poor health, he went to Africa to do missionary work and, as he said, to die. Strange to say, the hot climate and the African fever seemed to disturb him not at all; in fact, his health improved.

For twenty years, he remained there and preached to the people, and taught in the Liberian College. The natives often asked why he kept at his writing so closely. Later they discovered that he was writing a book called "The Future of Africa".

During his twenty years in Africa, he made only two visits to the United States. In 1873 he returned for good and took charge of an Episcopal Mission in Washington, D.C. He presided over this Mission, which developed into what is now St. Luke's Church, for twenty-two years. Often during these years, he went by invitation to the leading cities of the country, either to preach or to give lectures. In 1896, he founded "The American Negro Academy" at Washington, D.C., and gave some lectures before this organization.

He was a striking character, tall, erect and of noble carriage. He was dignified and fearless in manner, yet easy to approach.

During the last year of his life, he worked at his desk from six to seven hours every day, when he was able to write. Finally, for a little change, he went to Point Pleasant, New Jersey, and while there, passed away on the tenth of September, 1898. Just a few hours before his death, he dictated a letter to Paul Laurence Dunbar on the philosophy of poetry.

John Mercer Langston

Scholar and Congressman
1829-1897

John Mercer Langston was a frail child, only four years old, when his father and mother died. According to the will of his father, Captain Quarrels, he and his two brothers were to have all of their father's land, lying on Hickory Creek in Louisa County, Virginia. They were to have all of his stock of horses, cattle, sheep and bees, together with household and kitchen furniture and plantation utensils. They were also to have all of his money, in cash or in the form of debts due or bank stocks. Provision was made in Captain Quarrels's will for selling his property and dividing the money among John Mercer and his other boys, should they leave Louisa County.

The time came when this provision in the will was to be carried out. John Mercer and his brothers, with their attendants, remained in Louisa County two months after their father's death, getting ready to start for Ohio.

During this period of preparation, they secured the proper papers to take on such a journey. They and their attendants obtained a carry-all—a light wagon with horses and harness—and set out early one October morning, in 1834, to what was then known as a far-away state—Ohio. The road over which they traveled was mountainous and frequently broken by small swollen streams which they had to ford, and rivers which they had to cross by means of crude ferries. However, there seemed to be no cause for anxiety except for little, frail John Mercer.

They continued their journey for one week, traveling by day and pitching their tents at night. One evening while someone was unhitching the horses, and two of them were pitching the tent, and John Mercer and the rest of them were bringing water from a nearby stream, a man on horse back with saddle bags came down the highway. The older Langston boys, recognizing him as their half-brother, whom their father had sent to Ohio long before his death, ran to meet him. Little John Mercer, whom he had never seen before, he took up in his arms, caressed him and looked at him, saying, "My! but you are like my dear mother, Lucy Langston! You have in a marked degree her Indian family likeness!" All of the boys made their way to the tent. The night passed.

The next day as the party proceeded on its journey, the half-brother shortened the stirrup leathers of his saddle to fit John Mercer's legs, and put him in his saddle. John Mercer took hold of the bridle reins timidly, but soon began to knock his little legs against the sides of the horse, saying, "Get up, sir." At length, he seemed weary and was again taken into the battered carry-all. They traveled on for two weeks longer, until they reached Chillicothe, Ohio.

John Mercer was taken to the home of Colonel Gooch, who once on a visit to Captain Quarrels, had promised that when John Mercer came to Ohio he would care for him and educate him. John Mercer was given a hot bath, his clothing was changed, and a chair was placed at the table for him by the side of Mrs. Gooch. He ate heartily, romped and played, and grew rapidly under the kind treatment of the Gooch family. Soon he was known to the neighbors as "Johnnie Gooch".

Four years for him in the Gooch home passed. One beautiful Monday morning, in 1837, he, with his little new dinner-pail in one hand, and his book in the other, accompanied by Mr. Gooch, started out to school. Clad in his neat dress of round-about and pants of Kentucky blue jeans, he and Mr. Gooch trudged along until they reached the schoolhouse.

John Mercer was soon assigned to his class and his seat. As he sat upon the high seat without a back, he almost toppled over backwards. Then, apparently afraid of falling backwards, he leaned so far forward that he fell over on his nose. He twisted and turned on the tiresome seat for several days, then told his teacher that he was needed at home at two o'clock every day to drive up the cows. For one week he went home every day at two o'clock. Mr. Gooch asked the reason for John Mercer's early arrival home every day, and informed the teacher that John Mercer's whole business was to attend school.

Many agents were in Chillicothe at this time telling of the rich farm land in Missouri that could be bought very cheaply. The Gooch family was among the old residents who were selling out and preparing to leave for Missouri. They chartered a canal-boat and a steamboat for moving their things, and planned for a wagon and team to take the family across the country. Mr. Gooch called John Mercer in and asked if he wished to go with them. John Mercer replied, "I do, Colonel Gooch."

"Then you shall go," said the colonel.

When everything was in readiness, the family set out one night on their journey. The next morning, John Mercer spied two objects in the distance coming towards them. As they approached, he saw that they were two men, and one of them was his half-brother. The other gentleman made himself known at once as the sheriff, who had come to arrest Colonel Gooch for kidnapping John Mercer. Colonel Gooch, obeying orders, saddled his horse, took John Mercer up behind him and rode with the men back to Chillicothe. The court ruled that John Mercer should be left there.

Upon the advice of someone, he returned to the old Gooch home and farm, which were now in the hands of another. The first question the man asked was, "What, sir, can you do?"

John Mercer promptly answered, "I can't do anything."

The farmer then asked, "How do you expect to live? Get the horse and cart out and haul those bricks up from the distant field." John Mercer started forth to try to hitch the horse to the cart and to haul the bricks.

The third day, the farmer said, "You are doing well, and if you continue, you will make a good driver." The boy not only hauled bricks, but he plowed and hoed and became strong and healthy.

On leaving the farmer, he went to Cincinnati, Ohio, and secured work for afternoons and Saturdays, in a barber shop. Thus was he soon able to enter school in that city. One day as he sat with his class, studying his lesson, a man appeared at the door and asked for him. His teacher said, "John Mercer may go to the door. Someone wishes to see him." He arose and walked forth. At the sight of Colonel Gooch, who had sought him in Chillicothe and had come on to Cincinnati, he leaped out of the door and grasped his hand. They talked for a long, long time. Mr. Gooch kissed him good-bye, and John Mercer promised to join him in Missouri later on.

John Mercer's two years' stay in Cincinnati was interrupted by a call to Chillicothe, on business connected with his father's estate. While he was on this trip, he met an Oberlin College student who was teaching in Chillicothe, and who agreed to give him lessons. He studied under this teacher until his brothers agreed to send him to Oberlin College.

On Thursday morning, March 1, 1844, he and his teacher left Chillicothe for Oberlin. When they arrived the following Sunday morning, they saw hundreds of college students making their way through the muddy streets to early prayer service and Sunday School. Lodging for the night was secured in the only hotel then in Oberlin. The next day John Mercer registered and was taken to the home in which he was to live.

Seeing how busy every one about the college was, he secured his books and settled down to hard study. Before many weeks had passed, he was invited to join two college clubs—"The Young Men's Lyceum" and "The Union Society". Because of having friends in "the Union Society", he joined it, and was immediately called upon to take part in a debate.

On the evening of the debate, a very capable young man came forward as the first speaker. When he had finished, another young man was called forth. He, too, presented his side of the question in a convincing manner. John Mercer Langston was called upon as the third speaker. He came forward, took his place on the platform and said, "Mr. President—Mr. President." He stood there unable to say another word. Finally he rushed to his seat and began to cry. He wiped away the copious tears until his handkerchief, his cap and his coat sleeve were soaking wet. Then he hurried to his room, threw himself on the bed and cried until his pillow was wet through. The next morning, he arose with his face and eyes all swollen. As he stood before his little mirror, he held up his hands to God, with the vow that he would never fail again in making a speech. When friends sympathized with him, he said, "I thank you, but never mind."

After leaving breakfast, as John Mercer walked up the street, he met a friend who said he was called home. Immediately he asked John Mercer to take his place in the Society debate the next Thursday evening. He agreed at once and began to get ready for the debate. Thursday evening came; the hall was full of young men. When John Mercer was called forth, he took his place, addressed the presiding officer and spoke his ten minutes amid applause. Some young man called out, "Mr. President, I move by common consent that Langston be given ten minutes more." The motion was carried and Langston spoke ten minutes more, interrupted by frequent applause.

He remained in college to the end of the fall term, and returned to Chillicothe. No sooner had he arrived, than a committee called upon him to get him to teach school. Hicks Settlement, eight miles in the country, needed a teacher. The committee offered him ten dollars a month—and "board around". He accepted the position, although he was not quite sixteen years old. When he reached the schoolhouse the first morning, he says that he was more greatly surprised perhaps than anyone else, because he was smaller than any of the pupils except one.

"Boarding around" had its surprises, too. Every week he stayed with a different family, and each family tried to outdo the preceding ones in furnishing him good things to eat. Sometimes he just had to eat and eat until he felt like a stuffed goose. Finally he made arrangements with a man to give him and his son lessons and thereby obtain from them board and lodging for himself and his horse. At the end of every month, the school committee waited upon him and counted out to him his ten dollars in five and ten-cent pieces.

When Langston's three months at Hicks Settlement were up, he sat down with his bag of five- and ten-cent pieces and counted out the thirty dollars. Before many days had passed, he was on his way back to Oberlin College.

He entered and worked hard for four years, graduating at the age of twenty as a Bachelor of Arts— "B.A." He continued his studies at Oberlin and received his Master's degree—"M.A."

Three years later, he was graduated from the Oberlin Theological Seminary as a Bachelor of Divinity—"B.D." He remained in Oberlin and studied law under a prominent judge. When he had finished this course, he passed his examinations and under great odds was admitted to the bar in Ohio, where he practiced for a time and won notable cases.

He often said, in later years, that around Oberlin College centered many happy memories. He courted and married an Oberlin College girl by the name of Miss Wall. He settled in Oberlin and practiced law there until the bloody Civil War.

At that time, the United States was calling to her aid the ablest men she could find. John Mercer Langston was among those called. He responded immediately and began to travel over the West and the North getting men for the army. He secured them for three regiments the Fifty-fourth and Fifty-fifth Massachusetts and the Fifth United States of Ohio. After the war he continued to travel for the

Government for two years and a half, helping the people organize schools for their children.

When that work was finished, Howard University called him to organize her Law Department. For seven years he taught in that Department, and served for a time as Acting President of the University. He was admitted to practice law before the Supreme Court of the United States. And the President of the United States appointed him a member of the Board of Health of the District of Columbia.

Later on, another President appointed him Minister to Hayti, at a salary of $7,500 a year. After serving on that island for seven years, he returned to the United States and soon afterward was elected President of the Virginia State College at Petersburg. The state of Virginia claimed him as her own son. She honored him as a scholarly man. She elected him to the United States House of Representatives, in which he took his seat in 1890.

His last years were spent with his family at his home on College Street, Washington, District of Columbia. Before his death, November 15, 1897, he published a book of addresses called "Freedom and Citizenship".

Introduction

The Negro has been in America just about three hundred years and in that time he has become intertwined in all the history of the nation. He has fought in her wars; he has endured hardships with her pioneers; he has toiled in her fields and factories; and the record of some of the nation's greatest heroes is in large part the story of their service and sacrifice for this people.

The Negro arrived in America as a slave in 1619, just one year before the Pilgrims arrived at Plymouth in search of freedom. Since then their lot has not always been a happy one, but nevertheless, in spite of difficulties and hardships, the race has learned many valuable lessons in its conflict with the American civilization. As a slave the lessons of labor, of constructive endeavor, of home-life and religion were learned, even if the opportunity was not always present to use these lessons to good advantage.

After slavery other lessons were learned in their order. Devoted self-sacrificing souls—soldiers of human brotherhood—took up the task in the schoolroom which their brothers began on the battlefield. Here it was that the Negro learned the history of America, of the deeds of her great men, the stirring events which marked her development, the ideals that made America great. And so well have they been learned, that to-day there are no more loyal Americans than the twelve million Negroes that make up so large a part of the nation.

But the race has other things yet to learn: The education of any race is incomplete unless the members of that race know the history and character of its own people as well as those of other peoples. The Negro has yet to learn of the part which his own race has played in making America great; has yet to learn of the noble and heroic souls among his own people, whose achievements are praiseworthy among any people. A number of books—poetry, history and fiction—have been written by Negro authors in which the life of their own people has been faithfully and attractively set forth; but until recently no effort has been made on a large scale to see that Negro boys and girls became acquainted with these books and the facts they contained concerning their people.

In this volume the publishers have brought together a number of selections from the best literary works of Negro authors, through which these young people may learn more of the character and accomplishments of the worthy members of their race. Such matter is both informing and inspiring, and no Negro boy or girl can read it without feeling a deeper pride in his own race. The selections are each calculated to teach a valuable lesson, and all make a direct appeal to the best impulses of the human heart.

For a number of years several educational institutions for Negro youths have conducted classes in Negro history with a similar object in view. The results of these classes have been most gratifying and the present volume is a commendable contribution to the literature of such a course.

Robert R. Moton

Tuskegee Institute, Ala.,
June 30, 1920

To the man in the tower the world below him is likely to look very small. Men look like ants and all the bustle and stir of their hurrying lives seems pitifully confused and aimless. But the man in the street who is looking and striving upward is in a different situation. However poor his present plight, the thing he aims at and is striving toward stands out clear and distinct above him, inspiring him with hope and ambition in his struggle upward. For the man who is down there is always something to hope for, always something to be gained. The man who is down, looking up, may catch a glimpse now and then of heaven, but the man who is so situated that he can only look down is pretty likely to see another and quite different place.

BOOKER T. WASHINGTON

Going to School Under Difficulties

William H. Holtzclaw

When I was four years old I was put to work on the farm,—that is, at such work as I could do, such as riding a deaf and blind mule while my brother held the plow. When I was six years old my four-year-old brother and I had to go two miles through a lonely forest every morning in order to carry my father's breakfast and dinner to a sawmill, where he was hauling logs for sixty cents a day. The white man, Frank Weathers, who employed a large number of hands, both Negroes and whites, was considered one of the best and most upright men in that section of the country.

In those days there were no public schools in that part of the country for the Negroes. Indeed, public schools for whites were just beginning to be established. This man set aside a little house in the neighborhood of the sawmill, employed a teacher, and urged all the Negroes to send their children to this school. Not a great many of them, however, took advantage of his generosity, for this was at the time when everybody seemed to think that the Negro's only hope was in politics.

But my father and mother had great faith in education, and they were determined that their children should have that blessing of which they themselves had been deprived.

Soon, however, Mr. Weathers had cut all the timber that he could get in that section, and he therefore moved his mills to another district. This left us without a school. But my father was not to be outdone. He called a meeting of the men in that community, and they agreed to build a schoolhouse themselves. They went to the forest and cut pine poles about eight inches in diameter, split them in halves, and carried them on their shoulders to a nice shady spot, and there erected a little schoolhouse. The benches were made of the same material, and there was no floor nor chimney. Some of the other boys' trousers suffered when they sat on the new pine benches, which exuded rosin, but I had an advantage of them in this respect, for I wore only a shirt. In fact, I never wore trousers until I got to be so large that the white neighbors complained of my insufficient clothes.

At the end of the first school year there was a trying time in our family. On this occasion the teacher ordered all the pupils to appear dressed in white. We had no white clothes, nor many of any other sort, for that matter. Father and mother discussed our predicament nearly all one night. Father said it was foolish to buy clothes which could be used for that occasion only. But my ever resourceful mother was still determined that her children should look as well on this important occasion as any of our neighbors. However, when we went to bed the night before the exhibition we still had no white clothes and no cloth from which to make them. Nevertheless, when we awoke the next morning, all three of us had beautiful white suits.

It came about in this way. My mother had a beautiful white Sunday petticoat, which she had cut up and made into suits for us. As there is just so much cloth in a petticoat and no more, the stuff had to be cut close to cover all of us children, and as the petticoat had been worn several times and was, therefore, likely to tear, we had to be very careful how we stooped in moving about the stage, lest there should be a general splitting and tearing, with consequences that we were afraid to imagine. At the exhibitions the next night we said our little pieces, and

I suppose we looked about as well as the others; at least we thought so, and that was sufficient. One thing I am sure of,—there was no mother there who was prouder of her children than ours. The thing that made her so pleased was the fact that my speech made such an impression that our white landlord lifted me off the stage when I had finished speaking and gave me a quarter of a dollar.

If there happened to be a school in the winter time, I had sometimes to go bare-footed and always with scant clothing. Our landlady was very kind in such cases. She would give me clothes that had already been worn by her sons, and in turn I would bring broom straw from the sedges, with which she made her brooms. In this way I usually got enough clothes to keep me warm.

So, with my mother's encouragement, I went to school in spite of my bare feet. Often the ground would be frozen, and often there would be snow. My feet would crack and bleed freely, but when I reached home Mother would have a tub full of hot water ready to plunge me into and thaw me out. Although this caused my feet and legs to swell, it usually got me into shape for school the next day.

I remember once, when I had helped "lay by" the crops at home and was ready to enter the little one-month school, it was decided that I could not go, because I had no hat. My mother told me that if I could catch a 'coon and cure the skin, she would make me a cap out of that material. That night I went far into the forest with my hounds, and finally located a 'coon. The 'coon was a mighty fighter, and when he had driven off all my dogs I saw that the only chance for me to get a cap was to whip the 'coon myself, so together with the dogs I went at him, and finally we conquered him. The next week I went to school wearing my new 'coon-skin cap.

Exertions of this kind, from time to time, strengthened my will and my body, and prepared me for more trying tests which were to come later.

As I grew older it became more and more difficult for me to go to school. When cotton first began to open,—early in the fall,—it brought a higher price than at any other time of the year. At this time the landlord wanted us all to stop school and pick cotton. But Mother wanted me to remain in school, so, when the landlord came to the quarters early in the morning to stir up the cotton pickers, she used to out-general him by hiding me behind the skillets, ovens, and pots, throwing some old rags over me until he was gone. Then she would slip me off to school through the back way. I can see her now with her hands upon my shoulder, shoving me along through the woods and underbrush, in a roundabout way, keeping me all the time out of sight of the great plantation until we reached the point, a mile away from home, where we came to the public road. There my mother would bid me good-bye, whereupon she would return to the plantation and try to make up to the landlord for the work of us both in the field as cotton pickers.

The Beginnings of a Mississippi School

I had been unable to get permission to teach in the little church, so I started my school in the open air. We were out under the big trees amidst the shrubbery. This would have made a very good schoolhouse but for its size. In such a schoolhouse one could get along very well, if he could keep his pupils close enough to him, but the chances are, as I have found, that they will put bugs down one another's collars, and while you are hearing one class the other children will chase one another about. Their buoyant spirits will not permit them to keep quiet while they are in the open. It is pretty hard to hear a class reciting and at the same time to witness a boxing-match, but those who teach in the open air must be prepared for such performances. These annoyances were accentuated by the fact that some of my pupils were forty years old while others were six.

After a while we moved into an abandoned house, which we used for a schoolhouse, but it was little better than teaching out of doors. When it rained the water not only came through the roof, but through the sides as well. During cold winter rains I had to teach while standing with my overcoat on and with arctic rubbers to protect myself against pneumonia. During those rainy days Miss Lee, my assistant, would get up on a bench and stand there all day to keep her feet out of the water and would have an umbrella stretched over her to keep from getting wet from above. The little fellows would be standing in the water below like little ducks. They stood these conditions exceedingly well. Many of them were not protected with overshoes or any shoes, but they came to school each day just as if they had been properly clad.

It is impossible to describe the hardships that we suffered during that winter, which was severe for the South. As the winter came on and grew more and more severe a great many of the children were taken with pneumonia, la grippe, and similar ailments. I wished, in the interest of health, to abandon the school for a few weeks until better weather; but neither pupils, nor teachers, nor parents would listen to this, and so the school continued under these circumstances until the new schoolhouse was ready for use. It is needless to say that some of the pupils never survived those conditions; in fact, the strange thing is that any of us did.

My First School

W.E.B. Dubois

Once upon a time I taught school in the hills of
Tennessee, where the broad dark vale of the
Mississippi begins to roll and crumple to greet the
Alleghanies. I was a Fisk student then, and all Fisk
men thought that Tennessee—beyond the Veil—was
theirs alone, and in vacation time they sallied forth in
lusty bands to meet the county school-
commissioners. Young and happy, I too went, and I
shall not soon forget that summer.

First, there was a Teachers' Institute at the county-
seat; and there distinguished guests of the
superintendent taught the teachers fractions and
spelling and other mysteries,—white teachers in the
morning, Negroes at night. A picnic now and then,
and a supper, and the rough world was softened by
laughter and song. I remember how—but I wander.

There came a day when all the teachers left the
Institute and began the hunt for schools. I learn from
hearsay (for my mother was mortally afraid of
firearms) that the hunting of ducks and bears and men
is wonderfully interesting, but I am sure that the man

who has never hunted a country school has something to learn of the pleasures of the chase. I see now the white, hot roads lazily rise and fall and wind before me under the burning July sun; I feel the deep weariness of heart and limb as ten, eight, six miles stretch relentlessly ahead; I feel my heart sink heavily as I hear again and again, "Got a teacher? Yes." So I walked on—horses were too expensive—until I wandered beyond railways, beyond stage lines, to a land of "varmints" and rattlesnakes, where the coming of a stranger was an event, and men lived and died in the shadow of one blue hill.

Sprinkled over hill and dale lay cabins and farmhouses, shut out from the world by the forests and the rolling hills toward the east. There I found at last a little school. Josie told me of it; she was a thin, homely girl of twenty, with a dark-brown face and thick, hard hair. I had crossed the stream at Watertown, and rested under the great willows; then I had gone to the little cabin in the lot where Josie was resting on her way to town. The gaunt farmer made me welcome, and Josie, hearing my errand, told me anxiously that they wanted a school over the hill; that but once since the war had a teacher been there; that she herself longed to learn,—and thus she ran on, talking fast and loud, with much earnestness and energy.

Next morning I crossed the tall round hill, lingered to look at the blue and yellow mountains stretching toward the Carolinas, then plunged into the wood, and came out at Josie's home. It was a dull frame cottage with four rooms, perched just below the brow of the hill, amid peach trees. The father was a quiet, simple soul, calmly ignorant, with no touch of vulgarity. The mother was different,—strong, bustling, and energetic, with a quick, restless tongue, and an ambition to live "like folks."

There was a crowd of children. Two boys had gone away. There remained two growing girls; a shy midget of eight; John, tall, awkward, and eighteen; Jim, younger, quicker, and better looking; and two babies of indefinite age. Then there was Josie herself. She seemed to be the center of the family: always busy at service, or at home, or berry-picking; a little nervous and inclined to scold, like her mother, yet faithful, too, like her father. She had about her a certain fineness, the shadow of an unconscious moral heroism that would willingly give all of life to make life broader, deeper, and fuller for her and hers.

I saw much of this family afterwards, and grew to love them for their honest efforts to be decent and comfortable, and for their knowledge of their own ignorance. There was with them no affectation. The mother would scold the father for being so "easy"; Josie would roundly berate the boys for carelessness; and all know that it was a hard thing to dig a living out of a rocky side-hill.

I secured the school. I remember the day I rode horseback out to the commissioner's house with a pleasant young white fellow who wanted the white school. The road ran down the bed of a stream; the sun laughed and the water jingled, and we rode on. "Come in," said the commissioner,—"come in. Have a seat. Yes, that certificate will do. Stay to dinner. What do you want a month?" "Oh," thought I, "this is lucky"; but even then fell the first awful shadow of the Veil, for they ate first, then I—alone.

The schoolhouse was a log hut, where Colonel Wheeler used to shelter his corn. It sat in a lot behind a rail fence and thorn bushes, near the sweetest of springs. There was an entrance where a door once was, and within, a massive rickety fireplace; great chinks between the logs served as windows. Furniture was scarce. A pale blackboard crouched in the corner.

242

My desk was made of three boards, reinforced at critical points, and my chair, borrowed from the landlady, had to be returned every night. Seats for the children—these puzzled me much. I was haunted by a New England vision of neat little desks and chairs, but, alas! the reality was rough plank benches without backs, and at times without legs. They had the one virtue of making naps dangerous,—possibly fatal, for the floor was not to be trusted.

It was a hot morning late in July when the school opened. I trembled when I heard the patter of little feet down the dusty road, and saw the growing row of dark solemn faces and bright eager eyes facing me. First came Josie and her brothers and sisters. The longing to know, to be a student in the great school at Nashville, hovered like a star above this child-woman amid her work and worry, and she studied doggedly. There were the Dowells from their farm over toward Alexandria,—Fanny, with her smooth black face and wondering eyes; Martha, brown and dull; the pretty girl-wife of a brother, and the younger brood.

There were the Burkes,—two brown and yellow lads, and a tiny haughty-eyed girl. Fat Reuben's little chubby girl came, with golden face and old-gold hair, faithful and solemn. 'Thenie was on hand early,—a jolly, ugly, good-hearted girl, who slyly dipped snuff and looked after her little bow-legged brother. When her mother could spare her, 'Tildy came,—a midnight beauty, with starry eyes and tapering limbs; and her brother, correspondingly homely. And then the big boys,—the hulking Lawrences; the lazy Neills, unfathered sons of mother and daughter; Hickman, with a stoop in his shoulders; and the rest.

There they sat, nearly thirty of them, on the rough benches, their faces shading from a pale cream to a deep brown, the little feet bare and swinging, the eyes full of expectation, with here and there a twinkle of mischief, and the hands grasping Webster's blue-back spelling-book. I loved my school, and the fine faith the children had in the wisdom of their teacher was truly marvelous. We read and spelled together, wrote a little, picked flowers, sang, and listened to stories of the world beyond the hill.

At times the school would dwindle away, and I would start out. I would visit Mun Eddings, who lived in two very dirty rooms, and ask why little Lugene, whose flaming face seemed ever ablaze with the dark-red hair uncombed, was absent all last week, or why I missed so often the inimitable rags of Mack and Ed. Then the father, who worked Colonel Wheeler's farm on shares, would tell me how the crops needed the boys; and the thin, slovenly mother, whose face was pretty when washed, assured me that Lugene must mind the baby. "But we'll start them again next week." When the Lawrences stopped, I knew that the doubts of the old folks about book-learning had conquered again, and so, toiling up the hill, and getting as far into the cabin as possible, I put Cicero "pro Archia Poeta" into the simplest English with local applications, and usually convinced them—for a week or so.

On Friday nights I often went home with some of the children,—sometimes to Doc Burke's farm. He was a great, loud, thin Black, ever working, and trying to buy the seventy-five acres of hill and dale where he lived; but people said that he would surely fail, and the "white folks would get it all." His wife was a magnificent Amazon, with saffron face and shining hair, uncorseted and barefooted, and the children were strong and beautiful. They lived in a one-and-a-half-room cabin in the hollow of the farm, near the spring. The front room was full of great fat white beds, scrupulously neat; and there were bad chromos on the walls, and a tired center-table. In the tiny back kitchen I was often invited to "take out and help" myself to fried chicken and wheat biscuit, "meat" and corn pone, string-beans and berries.

At first I used to be a little alarmed at the approach of bedtime in the lone bedroom, but embarrassment was very deftly avoided. First, all the children nodded and slept, and were stowed away in one great pile of goose feathers; next, the mother and the father discreetly slipped away to the kitchen while I went to bed; then, blowing out the dim light, they retired in the dark. In the morning all were up and away before I thought of awaking. Across the road, where fat Reuben lived, they all went out-doors while the teacher retired, because they did not boast the luxury of a kitchen.

I liked to stay with the Dowells, for they had four rooms and plenty of good country fare. Uncle Bird had a small, rough farm, all woods and hills, miles from the big road; but he was full of tales,—he preached now and then,—and with his children, berries, horses, and wheat he was happy and prosperous. Often, to keep the peace, I must go where life was less lovely; for instance, 'Tildy's mother was incorrigibly dirty, Reuben's larder was limited seriously, and herds of untamed insects wandered over the Eddingses' beds. Best of all I loved to go to Josie's, and sit on the porch, eating peaches, while the mother bustled and talked: how Josie had bought the sewing-machine; how Josie worked at service in winter, but that four dollars a month was "mighty little" wages; how Josie longed to go away to school, but that it "looked like" they never could get far enough ahead to let her; how the crops failed and the well was yet unfinished; and, finally, how "mean" some of the white folks were.

For two summers I lived in this little world; it was dull and humdrum. The girls looked at the hill in wistful longing, and the boys fretted and haunted Alexandria. Alexandria was "town,"—a straggling, lay village of houses, churches, and shops, and an aristocracy of Toms, Dicks, and Captains. Cuddled on the hill to the north was the village of the colored folks, who lived in three- or four-room unpainted cottages, some neat and homelike, and some dirty. The dwellings were scattered rather aimlessly, but they centered about the twin temples of the hamlet, the Methodist and the Hard-Shell Baptist churches. These, in turn, leaned gingerly on a sad-colored schoolhouse. Hither my little world wended its crooked way on Sunday to meet other worlds, and gossip, and wonder, and make the weekly sacrifice with frenzied priest at the altar of the "old-time religion." Then the soft melody and mighty cadences of Negro song fluttered and thundered.

I have called my tiny community a world, and so its isolation made it; and yet there was among us but a half-awakened common consciousness, sprung from common joy and grief, at burial, birth, or wedding; from a common hardship in poverty, poor land, and low wages; and above all, from the sight of the Veil that hung between us and Opportunity. All this caused us to think some thoughts together; but these, when ripe for speech, were spoken in various languages. Those whose eyes twenty-five or more years before had seen "the glory of the coming of the Lord," saw in every present hindrance or help a dark fatalism bound to bring all things right in His own good time. The mass of those to whom slavery was a dim recollection of childhood found the world a puzzling thing: it asked little of them, and they answered with little, and yet it ridiculed their offering. Such a paradox they could not understand, and therefore sank into listless indifference, or shiftlessness, or reckless bravado. There were, however, some—such as Josie, Jim and Ben—to whom War, Hell, and Slavery were but childhood tales, whose young appetites had been whetted to an edge by school and story and half-awakened thought. Ill could they be content, born without and beyond the World. And their weak wings beat against their barriers,—barriers of caste, of youth, of life; at last, in dangerous moments, against everything that opposed even a whim.

The Colored Cadet at West Point

Lieut. Henry Ossian Flipper, U.S.A.

May 20th, 1873! Auspicious day! From the deck of the little ferry-boat that steamed its way across from Garrison's on that eventful afternoon I viewed the hills about West Point, her stone structures perched thereon, thus rising still higher, as if providing access to the very pinnacle of fame, and shuddered. With my mind full of the horrors of the treatment of all former cadets of color, and the dread of inevitable ostracism, I approached tremblingly yet confidently.

The little vessel having been moored, I stepped ashore and inquired of a soldier there where candidates should report. He very kindly gave me all information, wished me much success, for which I thanked him, and set out for the designated place. I soon reached it, and walked directly into the adjutant's office. He received me kindly, asked for my certificate of appointment, and receiving that—or assurance that I had it—I do not remember which—directed me to write in a book there for the purpose the name and occupation of my father, the State, Congressional district, county and city of his residence, my own full name, age, State, county, and place of my birth, and my occupation when at home. This done I was sent in charge of an orderly to cadet barracks, where my "plebe quarters" were assigned me.

The impression made upon me by what I saw while going from the adjutant's office to barracks was certainly not very encouraging. The rear windows were crowded with cadets watching my unpretending passage of the area of barracks with apparently as much astonishment and interest as they would, perhaps, have watched Hannibal crossing the Alps. Their words and jeers were most insulting.

Having reached another office, I was shown in by the orderly. I walked in, hat in hand—nay, rather started in—when three cadets, who were seated in the room, simultaneously sprang to their feet and welcomed me somewhat after this fashion:

"Well, sir, what do you mean by coming into this office in that manner, sir? Get out of here, sir."

I walked out, followed by one of them, who, in a similar strain, ordered me to button my coat, get my hands around—"fins" he said—heels together, and head up.

"Now, sir," said he, leaving me, "when you are ready to come in, knock at that door," emphasizing the word "knock."

The door was open. I knocked. He replied, "Come in." I went in. I took my position in front of and facing him, my heels together, head up, the palms of my hands to the front, and my little fingers on the seams of my pantaloons, in which position we habitually carried them. After correcting my position and making it sufficiently military to suit himself, one of them, in a much milder tone, asked what I desired of them. I told him I had been sent by the adjutant to report there. He arose, and directing me to follow him, conducted me to the bath-rooms. Having discharged the necessary duty there, I returned and was again put in charge of the orderly, who carried me to the hospital. There I was subjected to a rigid physical examination, which I "stood" with the greatest ease. I was given a certificate of ability by the surgeon, and by him sent again to the adjutant, who in turn sent me to the treasurer. From him I returned alone to barracks.

The reception given to "plebes" upon reporting is often very much more severe than that given me. Even members of my own class can testify to this. This reception has, however, I think, been best described in an anonymous work, where it is thus set forth:

"How dare you come into the presence of your superior officer in that grossly careless and unmilitary manner? I'll have you imprisoned. Stand, attention, sir!" (Even louder than before.) "Heels-together-and-on-the-same-line, toes-equally-turned-out, little-fingers-on-the-seams-of-your-pantaloons, button-your-coat, draw-in-your-chin, throw-out-your-chest, cast-your-eyes-fifteen-paces-to-the-front, don't-let-me-see-you-wearing-standing-collars-again. Stand-steady, sir. You've evidently mistaken your profession, sir. In any other service, or at the seat of war, sir, you would have been shot, sir, without trial, sir, for such conduct, sir."

The effect of such words can be easily imagined. A "plebe" will at once recognize the necessity for absolute obedience, even if he does know all this is hazing, and that it is doubtless forbidden. Still "plebes" almost invariably tremble while it lasts, and when in their own quarters laugh over it, and even practise it upon each other for mutual amusement.

On the way to barracks I met the squad of "beasts" marching to dinner. I was ordered to fall in, did so, marched to the mess hall, and ate my first dinner at

West Point. After dinner we were again marched to barracks and dismissed. I hastened to my quarters, and a short while after was turned out to take possession of my baggage. I lugged it into my room, was shown the directions on the back of the door for arrangement of articles, and ordered to obey them within half an hour.

At the end of the time specified every article was arranged and the cadet corporal returned to inspect. He walked deliberately to the clothes-press, and, informing me that everything was arranged wrong, threw every article upon the floor, repeated his order and withdrew. And thus three times in less than two hours did I arrange and he disarrange my effects. I was not troubled again by him till after supper, when he inspected again, merely opening the door, however, and looking in. He told me I could not go to sleep till "tattoo." Now tattoo, as he evidently used it, referred in some manner to time, and with such reference I had not the remotest idea of what it meant. I had no knowledge whatever of military terms or customs. However, as I was also told that I could do anything— writing, etc.—I might wish to do, I found sufficient to keep me awake until he again returned and told me it was then tattoo, that I could retire then or at any time within half an hour, and that at the end of that time the light *must* be extinguished and I *must* be in bed. I instantly extinguished it and retired.

Thus passed my first half day at West Point, and thus began the military career of the fifth colored cadet. The other four were Smith of South Carolina, Napier of Tennessee, Howard of Mississippi, and Gibbs of Florida.

A Negro Explorer at the North Pole
Matthew A. Henson

"Matthew A. Henson, my Negro assistant, has been with me in one capacity or another since my second trip to Nicaragua in 1887. I have taken him on each and all of my expeditions, except the first, and also without exception on each of my farthest sledge trips. This position I have given him primarily because of his adaptability and fitness for the work and secondly on account of his loyalty. He is a better dog driver and can handle a sledge better than any man living, except some of the best Esquimo hunters themselves.

"Robert E. Peary, Rear Admiral, U. S. N."

Exactly 40° below zero when we pushed the sledges up to the curled-up dogs and started them off over rough ice covered with deep soft snow. It was like walking in loose granulated sugar. Indeed I might compare the snow of the Arctic to the granules of sugar, without their saccharine sweetness, but with freezing cold instead; you cannot make snowballs of it, for it is too thoroughly congealed, and when it is packed by the wind it is almost as solid as ice. It is from the packed snow that the blocks used to form the igloo-walls are cut.

At the end of four hours, we came to the igloo where the Captain and his boys were sleeping the sleep of utter exhaustion. In order not to interrupt the Captain's rest, we built another igloo and unloaded his sledge, and distributed the greater part of the load among the sledges of the party. The Captain, on awakening, told us that the journey we had completed on that day had been made by him under the most trying conditions, and that it had taken him fourteen hours to do it. We were able to make better time because we had his trail to follow, and, therefore, the necessity of finding the easiest way was avoided. That was the object of the scout or pioneer party and Captain Bartlett had done practically all of it up to the time he turned back at 87° 48' north.

March 29, 1909: You have undoubtedly taken into consideration the pangs of hunger and of cold that you know assailed us, going Poleward; but have you ever considered that we were thirsty for water to drink or hungry for fat? To eat snow to quench our thirsts would have been the height of folly, and as well as being thirsty, we were continually assailed by the pangs of a hunger that called for the fat, good, rich, oily, juicy fat that our systems craved and demanded.

Had we succumbed to the temptations of the thirst and eaten the snow, we would not be able to tell the tale of the conquest of the Pole; for the result of eating snow is death. True, the dogs licked up enough moisture to quench their thirsts, but we were not made of such stern stuff as they. Snow would have reduced our temperatures and we would quickly have fallen by the way. We had to wait until camp was made and the fire of alcohol started before we had a chance, and it was with hot tea that we quenched our thirsts. The hunger for fat was not appeased; a dog or two was killed, but his carcass went to the Esquimos and the entrails were fed to the rest of the pack.

April 1, the Farthest North of Bartlett: I knew at this time that he was to go back, and that I was to continue, so I had no misgivings and neither had he. He was ready and anxious to take the back-trail. His five marches were up and he was glad of it, and he was told that in the morning he must turn back and knit the trail together, so that the main column could return over a beaten path.

He swept his little party together and at three P.M., with a cheery "Good-by! Good Luck!" he was off. His Esquimo boys, attempting English, too, gave us their "Good-bys."

The Captain had gone. Commander Peary and I were alone (save for the four Esquimos), the same we had been with so often in the past years, and as we looked at each other we realized our position and we knew without speaking that the time had come for us to demonstrate that we were the men who, it had been ordained, should unlock the door which held the mystery of the Arctic. Without an instant's hesitation, the order to push on was given, and we started off in the trail made by the Captain to cover the Farthest North he had made and to push on over one hundred and thirty miles to our final destination.

Day and night were the same. My thoughts were on the going and getting forward, and on nothing else. The wind was from the southeast, and seemed to push on, and the sun was at our backs, a ball of livid fire, rolling his way above the horizon in never-ending day.

With my proven ability in gauging distances, Commander Peary was ready to take the reckoning as I made it and he did not resort to solar observations until we were within a hand's grasp of the Pole.

The memory of those last five marches, from the Farthest North of Captain Bartlett to the arrival of our party at the Pole, is a memory of toil, fatigue, and exhaustion, but we were urged on and encouraged by our relentless commander, who was himself being scourged by the final lashings of the dominating influence that had controlled his life. From the land to 87° 48' north, Commander Peary had had the best of the going, for he had brought up the rear and had utilized the trail made by the preceding parties, and thus he had kept himself in the best of condition for the time when he made the spurt that brought him to the end of the race. From 87° 48' north, he kept in the lead and did his work in such a way as to convince me that he was still as good a man as he had ever been. We marched and marched, falling down in our tracks repeatedly, until it was impossible to go on. We were forced to camp, in spite of the impatience of the Commander, who found himself unable to rest, and who only waited long enough for us to relax into sound sleep, when he would wake us up and start us off again. I do not believe that he slept for one hour from April 2 until after he had loaded us up and ordered us to go back over our old trail, and I often think that from the instant when the order to return was given until the land was again sighted, he was in a continual daze.

Onward we forced our weary way. Commander Peary took his sights from the time our chronometer-watches gave, and I, knowing that we had kept on going in practically a straight line, was sure that we had more than covered the necessary distance to insure our arrival at the top of the earth.

It was during the march of the 3d of April that I endured an instant of hideous horror. We were crossing a lane of moving ice. Commander Peary was in the lead setting the pace, and a half hour later the four boys and myself followed in single file. They had all gone before, and I was standing and pushing at the upstanders of my sledge, when the block of ice I was using as a support slipped from underneath my feet, and before I knew it the sledge was out of my grasp, and I was floundering in the water of the lead. I did the best I could. I tore my hood from off my head and struggled frantically. My hands were gloved and I could not take hold of the ice, but before I could give the "Grand Hailing Sigh of Distress," faithful old Ootah had grabbed me by the nape of the neck, the same as he would have grabbed a dog, and with one hand he pulled me out of the water, and with the other hurried the team across.

He had saved my life, but I did not tell him so, for such occurrences are taken as part of the day's work, and the sledge he safeguarded was of much more importance, for it held, as part of its load, the Commander's sextant, the mercury, and the coils of piano-wire that were the essential portion of the scientific part of the expedition. My kamiks (boots of sealskin) were stripped off, and the congealed water was beaten out of my bearskin trousers, and with a dry pair of kamiks, we hurried on to overtake the column. When we caught up, we found the boys gathered around the Commander, doing their best to relieve him of his discomfort, for he had fallen into the water, also, and while he was not complaining, I was sure that his bath had not been any more voluntary than mine had been.

It was about ten or ten-thirty A.M., on the 7th of April, 1909, that the Commander gave the order to build a snow-shield to protect him from the flying drift of the surface-snow. I knew that he was about to take an observation, and while we worked I was nervously apprehensive, for I felt that the end of our journey had come. When we handed him the pan of mercury the hour was within a very few minutes of noon. Lying flat on his stomach, he took the elevation and made the notes on a piece of tissue-paper at his head. With sun-blinded eyes, he snapped shut the vernier (a graduated scale that subdivides the smallest divisions on the sector of the circular scale of the sextant) and with the resolute squaring of his jaws, I was sure that he was satisfied, and I was confident that the journey had ended.

The Commander gave the word, "We will plant the Stars and Stripes—*at the North Pole!*" and it was done; on the peak of a huge paleo-crystic floeberg the glorious banner was unfurled to the breeze, and as it snapped and crackled with the wind, I felt a savage joy and exultation. Another world's accomplishment was done and finished, and as in the past, from the beginning of history, wherever the world's work was done by a white man, he had been accompanied by a colored man. From the building of the pyramids and the journey to the Cross, to the discovery of the North Pole, the Negro had been the faithful and constant companion of the Caucasian, and I felt all that it was possible for me to feel, that it was I, a lowly member of my race, who had been chosen by fate to represent it, at this, almost the last of the world's great work.

Negro Music That Stirred France

Emmett J. Scott

"You cannot defeat a singing nation," a keen-witted observer has said, in noting the victory spirit engendered by the martial music, the patriotic songs and the stirring melodies of hearth and home that have moved the souls of men to action on all the battlefields of history.

"Send me more singing regiments," cabled General Pershing, and Admiral Mayo sent frequent requests that a song leader organize singing on every battleship of the Atlantic Fleet.

Since "the morning stars sang together" in Scriptural narrative, music has exerted a profound influence upon mankind, be it in peace or in war, in gladness or in sorrow, or in the tender sentiment that makes for love of country, affection for kindred or the divine passion for "ye ladye fair." Music knows no land or clime, no season or circumstance, and no race, creed or clan. It speaks the language universal, and appeals to all peoples with a force irresistible and no training in ethics or science is necessary to reach the common ground that its philosophy instinctively creates in the human understanding.

The War Department was conscious of this and gave practical application to its theory that music makes a soldier "fit to fight" when it instituted, through the Commission on Training Camp Activities, a systematic program of musical instruction throughout the American Army at the home cantonments and followed up the work overseas. It was the belief that every man became a better warrior for freedom when his mind could be diverted from the dull routine of camp life by arousing his higher nature by song, and that he fared forth to battle with a stouter heart when his steps were attuned to the march by bands that drove out all fear of bodily danger and robbed "grim-visaged war" of its terrors. Skilled song leaders were detailed to the various camps and cantonments here and abroad, and bands galore were brought into service for inspiration and cheer.

The emotional nature of the Negro fitted him for this musical program. The colored American was a "close up" in every picture from the start to the finish and was a conspicuous figure in every scenario, playing with credit and distinction alike in melody or with the musket.

No instrumentality was more potent than music in off-setting the propaganda of the wily German agents, who sought to break down the loyalty of the Negro. The music he knew was intensely American—in sentiment and rhythm. It saturated his being—and all the blandishments of the enemy were powerless to sway him from the flag he loved. His grievances were overshadowed by the realization that the welfare of the nation was menaced and that his help was needed. American music harmonized with the innate patriotism of the race, and the majestic sweep of "The Star-Spangled Banner" or the sympathetic appeal of "My Country, 'Tis of Thee," were sufficient to counteract the sinister efforts of the missionaries of the Hohenzollerns to move him from his moorings.

No labor is ever so onerous that it can bar music from the soul of black folk. This race sings at work, at play and in every mood. Visitors to any army camp found the Negro doing musical "stunts" of some kind from reveille to taps—every hour, every minute of the day. All the time the trumpeters were not blowing out actual routine bugle calls, they were somewhere practicing them. Mouth-organs were going, concertinas were being drawn back and forth, and guitars, banjos, mandolins and whatnot were in use— playing all varieties of music, from the classic, like "Lucia," "Poet and Peasant," and "Il Trovatore" to the folksongs and the rollicking "Jazz." Music is indeed the chiefest outlet of the Negro's emotions, and the state of his soul can best be determined by the type of melody he pours forth.

Some writer has said that a handful of pipers at the head of a Scotch regiment could lead that regiment down the mouth of a cannon. It is not doubted that a Negro regiment could be made to duplicate the "Charge of the Light Brigade" at Balaklava—"into the mouth of hell," as Tennyson puts it—if one of their regimental bands should play—as none but a colored band can play—the vivacious strains of "There'll Be a Hot Time in the Old Town Tonight."

The Negro's love of home is an integral part of his nature, and is exemplified in the themes he plaintively crooned in camp on both sides of the ocean. Such melodies as "Carry Me Back to Old Virginia," "My Old Kentucky Home," "In the Evening by de Moonlight," and "Swanee River" recalled memories of the "old folks at home," and kept his patriotism alive, for he hoped to return to them some day and swell their hearts with pride by reason of the glorious record he made at the front.

The Negro is essentially religious, and his deep spiritual temperament is vividly illustrated by the joy he finds in "harmonizing" such ballads of ancient days as "Swing Low, Sweet Chariot," "Steal Away to Jesus," "Standin' in the Need of Prayer," "Every Time I Feel the Spirit," "I Wan' to be Ready," and "Roll, Jordan, Roll." The Negro is also an optimist, whether he styles himself by that high-sounding title or not, and the sincerity of his "make the best of it" disposition is noted in the fervor he puts into those uplifting gems, "Pack Up Your Troubles in Your Old Kit Bag and Smile, Smile, Smile," "There's a Long, Long Trail," "Keep the Home Fires Burning," and "Good-bye Broadway, Hello France."

Just as the Negro folk-songs—or songs of war, interpreted with the characteristic Negro flavor—stirred all France and gave poilu and populace a taste of the real American music, the marvelous "jazz bands" kept their feet patting and their shoulders "eagle-rocking" to its infectious motion. High officials are said to have been literally "carried away" with the "jazz" music furnished by the colored bands "over there" during the war. General Petain is said to have paid a visit, at the height of the hostilities, to a sector in which there were American troops and had "the time of his life" listening to a colored band playing the entrancing "jazz" music, with some Negro dance stunts in keeping with the spirit of the melodies. He warmly congratulated the colored leader upon the excellence of the work of his organization, and thanked him for the enjoyable entertainment that had been given him.

The stolid Briton is scarcely less susceptible to the "jazz" than his volatile French brother, for when another colored band from "The States" went to London to head a parade of American and English soldiers, and halted at Buckingham Palace, it is said that King George V and Queen Mary heard the lively airs with undisguised enthusiasm and were loath to have the players depart for the park where they were scheduled for a concert, with a dance engagement, under British military control, to follow. The colored bands scored heavily with the three great Allied Powers of Europe by rendering with a brilliant touch and matchless finish their national anthems, "God Save the Queen," "La Marseillaise" and the "Marcia Reale."

NOVEMBER 11, 1918

(This letter was written by a young first lieutenant (colored) in the 366th Infantry, Company L, 92nd Division, Cleveland, Ohio.)

November 11th.

My dearest Mother and Dad:

Well, folks, it's all over but the flowers. Yesterday it was war, hard, gruelling, hideous. Today it is peace.

This morning I formed my platoon in line in the woods behind the line. They didn't know why. They were just a bunch of tired, hard-bitten, mud-spattered, rough-and-tumble soldiers standing stoically at attention, equally ready to go over the top, rebuild a shell-torn road, or march to a rest billet. At 10:45 I gave the command: "Unload rifles!" They didn't know why and didn't particularly care. Then— "Unload pistols." And while they still stood rigid and motionless as graven images, I read the order declaring armistice and cessation of hostilities effective at 11 o'clock. The perfect discipline of these veteran soldiers held them still motionless, but I could see their eyes begin to shine and their muscles to quiver as the import of this miraculous message began to dawn on them.

The tension was fast straining their nerves to the breaking-point, so I dismissed them. You should have seen them! They yelled till they were hoarse. Some sang. Others, war-hardened veterans, who had faced the death hail of a machine-gun with a laugh, men who had gone through the horrors of artillery bombardments and had seen their fellows mangled and torn without a flinch, broke down and cried like babies.

Tonight something is wrong. The silence is almost uncanny. Not a shot—not even a single shell. Very faintly we can hear the mellow tones of the church bell in the little French town on the hill far to our rear. All day long it has been singing its song of joy and thanksgiving. It seems symbolical of the heart of France, which, today, is ringing.

I don't know when I'm coming home, but when I do, I want a big roast turkey, golden brown, new spuds swimming in butter and cranberry sauce.

Love,

Jesse.

How Two Colored Captains Fell

Ralph W. Tyler

A colored unit was ordered to charge, and take, if possible, a very difficult objective held by the Germans. Captains Fairfax and Green, two colored officers, were in command of the detachments. They made the charge, running into several miles of barb-wire entanglements, and hampered by a murderous fire from nests of German machine guns which were camouflaged.

Just before charging, one of the colored sergeants, running up to Captain Fairfax, said: "Do you know there is a nest of German machine guns ahead?"

The Captain replied: "I only know we have been ordered to go forward, and we are going."

Those were the last words he said, before giving the command to charge, "into the jaws of death." The colored troops followed their intrepid leader with all the enthusiasm and dash characteristic of patriots and courageous fighters. They went forward, they obeyed the order, and as a result sixty-two men and two officers were listed in the casualties reported.

Captain Fairfax's last words, "I only know we have been ordered to go forward, and we are going," are words that will forever live in the memory of his race; they are words that match those of Sergeant Carney, the color sergeant of the 54th Massachusetts during the Civil War, who, although badly wounded, held the tattered, shot-pierced Stars and Stripes aloft and exclaimed, "The old flag never touched the ground!"

Men who have served under Captains Fairfax and Green say two braver officers never fought and fell.

Ira Aldridge

The name of Aldridge has always been placed at the head of the list of Negro actors. He has indeed become the most noted of them, and his name is cited as standing first in his calling among all colored persons who have ever appeared on the stage. He was born at Belaire, near Baltimore, in 1804. In complexion he was dark brown, and with heavy whiskers; standing six feet in height, with heavy frame, African features, and yet with due proportions; he was graceful in his attitudes, highly polished in manners.

In his early days he was apprenticed to a ship carpenter, and had his association with the Germans on the western shores of Maryland. Here he became familiar with the German language and spoke it not only with ease but with fluency. He was brought in contact with Edmund Kean, the great actor, in 1826, whom he accompanied in his trip through Europe. His ambition to become an actor was encouraged by Kean, and receiving his assistance in the preparation, he made his appearance first at the Royalty Theatre in London, in the character of Othello. Public applause greeted him of such an extraordinary nature, that he was billed to appear at the Covent Garden Theatre April 10, 1839, in the same character.

After many years' successful appearances in many of the metropolitan cities, he appeared in the Provinces with still greater success. In Ireland he performed Othello, with Edmund Kean as Iago. In 1852 he appeared in Germany in Shakespearean characters. He was pronounced excellent, and though a stranger and a foreigner, he undertook the very difficult task of playing in English, while his whole support was rendered in the language of the country. It is said that until this time, such an experiment was not considered susceptible of a successful end, but nevertheless, with his impersonations he succeeded admirably. It is said that the King of Prussia was so deeply moved with his appearance in the character of Othello, at Berlin, that he sent him a congratulatory letter, and conferred upon him the title of chevalier, in recognition of his dramatic genius, and informed him that the lady who took the part of Desdemona was so much affected at the manner in which he played his part that she was made ill from fright on account of the reality with which he acted his part.

Some idea of the character of his acting might be gained from the fact that the lady who played

Desdemona in St. Petersburg, became very much alarmed at what appeared real passion on his part, in acting Othello; though he was never rough or indelicate in any of his acting with ladies, yet she was so frightened that she used to scream with real fear.

It is said that on another occasion in St. Petersburg, that in the midst of his acting in scene two, act five, when he was quoting these words,

"It is the cause, it is the cause, my soul;
 Let me not name it to you, you chaste stars!
 It is the cause. Yet I'll not shed her blood,
 Nor scar that whiter skin of hers than snow,
 And smooth as monumental alabaster.
 Yet she must die, else she'll betray more men.
 Put out the light, and then—put out the light!
 If I quench thee, thou flaming minister,
 I can again thy former light restore,
 Should I repent me: But once put out thy light,
 Thou cunning'st pattern of excelling nature;
 I know not where is that Promethean heat,
 That can thy light relume. When I have plucked
   thy rose,
 I cannot give it vital growth again;
 It needs must wither:—I'll smell it on the tree—
   (kissing her)

O balmy breath, that dost almost persuade
Justice to break her sword:—One more, one
    more:—
Be thus when thou art dead, and I will kill thee,
And love thee after:—One more—and this the
    last:
So sweet was ne'er so fatal. I must weep.
But they are cruel tears:
This sorrow's heavenly:
It strikes where it doth love."

the house was so carried away with the manner in
which he rendered it, that a young man stood up and
exclaimed with the greatest earnestness: "She is
innocent, Othello, she is innocent," and yet so
interested was he in the acting himself that he never
moved a muscle but continued as if nothing had been
said to embarrass him. The next day he learned, while
dining with a Russian prince, that a young man who
had been present had been so affected by the play that
he had been seized with a sudden illness and died the
next day.

Mr. Aldridge was a welcome guest in the ranks of
the cultured and wealthy, and was often in the
"salons" of the haughty aristocrats of St. Petersburg
and Moscow. Titled ladies wove, knitted and stitched

their pleasing emotions into various memorials of friendship. In his palatial residence at Sydenham, near London, were collected many presents of intrinsic value, rendered almost sacred by association. Prominent among these tokens of regard was an autographic letter from the King of Prussia, transmitting the first medal of art and sciences; the Cross of Leopold, from the Emperor of Russia, and a Maltese cross received at Berne.

In all his triumphs he never lost interest in the condition of his race. He always took an interest in everything touching their welfare, and though exalted to the companionship of those who ranked high in every department of life, yet he never in any way forgot the humble race with which he was identified, and was always solicitous for their welfare and promotion. He was an associate of the most prominent men of Paris, among whom was Alexander Dumas. When the great tragedian and great writer met they always kissed each other, and Dumas always greeted Aldridge with the words Mon Confrère. He died at Lodes, in Poland, August 7, 1867.

Out of Africa

About the year 1735 a fierce battle was waged between two strong tribes on the west coast of Africa. The chief of one of these tribes was counted among the most powerful of his time. This chief overpowered his rival and slaughtered and captured a great number of his band. Some of the captives escaped, others died, others still committed suicide, till but few were left. The victorious chief delivered to his son about a dozen of this forlorn remnant, and he, with an escort, took them away to be sold into slavery. The young African pushed his way through the jungle with his bodyguard until he reached the coast. Arrived there, he sold his captives to the captain of an American slave ship and received his pay in trinkets of various kinds, common to the custom of the trade. Then he was asked to row out in a boat and inspect the wonderful ship. He went, and with the captain and the crew saw every part of the vessel. When it was all over they offered him food and he ate it heartily. After that he remembered no more till he woke to find himself in the hold of the ship chained to one of the miserable creatures whom he himself had so recently sold as a slave, and the vessel itself was far beyond the sight of land.

After many days the ship arrived at the shores of America; the human cargo was brought to Richmond and this African slave merchant was sold along with his captives at public auction in the slave markets of the city. He was bought by a tobacco planter and carried to Amelia County, Virginia, where he lived to be a very old man. This man was my grandmother's great-grandfather.

According to the story as he told it to my grandmother, he brought more at auction than any other member of the party. He was a very fine specimen of physical manhood, weighing somewhere around two hundred pounds, and standing about six feet two inches in height. My grandmother said of him that he learned very little of the English language and used that little always with a pronounced foreign accent. He never grew to like America or Americans, white or black; and certain days, after the passing of so many moons, he observed religiously throughout his life. These were feast days with certain ceremonies of their own, in which, when possible, two other members of that same party though not of his tribe would join him. Each understood the tribal language of the others. These days, so my grandmother said, which occurred about three times a year, his owner permitted him to take off, leaving him undisturbed, for at other times he was entirely faithful and conscientious in his work. His great-granddaughter—my mother's mother—was not, I should judge, very unlike this great-great-great grandfather of mine, for in her youth she was a magnificent type of womanhood, both physically and mentally; and even to her death, at ninety-six years of age, she was possessed of remarkable physical and mental vigour. She "carried the keys" on her owner's, Doctor Craddock's, plantation, and stood next on the female side of the household to his wife, superintending the making of the clothes, caring for the children on the plantation, and in later years conducting what would in the present day be called a Day Nursery; that is, caring for the children of the mothers who were in the field, seeing to their food and dress, and to their conduct, of course. Frequently these old mothers were very clever in story telling, so that "Uncle Remus," "Brer Fox," and "Brer Rabbit" were familiar to the children of the South, both white and black, many years before they got into print.

My father's mother, who lived to be 108 years old, was also brought directly from Africa, and was finally sold to a planter who lived in Charlotte County, Virginia. It was there my father was born. He was owned by Doctor Alexander of that county, and when he died, about 1850, and the estate was divided, my father was sold to John Crowder of Prince Edward County, and, I think, presented to his wife as a Christmas present. I have many times heard my father tell of his experiences as a slave; of the many hardships through which he passed, and of the many good times he had even as a slave, for one of the fortunate traits of the Negro is his jovial nature, his ability to see humour even in adversity, and to laugh and sing under almost any circumstances. I have often thought that most other races, had they gone through the difficulties which the Negro faced, would have produced much more insanity than has been found in the past among Negroes; unfortunately, however, insanity is increasing very much indeed among my people, an indication in all probability that they are taking life much more seriously than they have done in the past.

There were many kind masters during slavery days; and there must have been such a thing as kindness even between master and slave. The overseers who were generally of the poorer class of white people were, as a rule, the cause of much of the contention and usually made most of the trouble; at least the Negroes thought so. They were night patrollers, or, as the Negroes called them, "patter-rollers," and were paid by the hour in many places to catch and whip any slave found off his master's plantation after nightfall without a pass. Not infrequently these people received from the master class less consideration even than the slave, and in most cases the bitterest animosity and hatred existed between the overseers and the slaves. It was not unusual that Negroes considered themselves superior in every respect to the overseer class, whose members were generally referred to among them as "po'h white trash." This expression was "the last word" in degradation, infamy, and general contempt that Negroes could command. Even to-day, when Negroes refer to people as "poor white trash," it has a meaning all its own, and I am of the opinion that much of the ill feeling between the races in our country to-day had its origin in these unpleasant relations between overseer and slaves before Emancipation.

On the Crowder plantation there was an overseer who had a particular dislike for my father, probably because he thought that my father received entirely too much consideration from his master and mistress; in short, there was a kind of jealous rivalry between them. It is unnecessary to say that the dislike on the part of the overseer was generously reciprocated by my father. If there was any difference, it was that the hatred on my father's part was the stronger—if that were possible; and without doubt, being in the confidence of his master, he used his opportunity to the disadvantage of the overseer. It was the rule of the plantation that no slaves except such as the master designated should be whipped by the overseer. My father, of course, was thus exempted. On one occasion the overseer, unfortunately, and against the order of his employer, insisted upon whipping my father. The scene took place in a tobacco barn where my father was engaged with perhaps fifty other slaves in sorting and stripping tobacco. In the scuffle, in which several other slaves helped the overseer in response to his call, my father easily got the upper hand, for he was a man of unusual strength. He not only overpowered the overseer but the men who undertook to assist him, maiming the overseer and one of the men very seriously. This was in the midst of a severe snow storm. My father took the only course, as it seemed, that was open to "obstreperous" slaves—he took to the woods. This was in early December. Here he remained, picking up what food he could at nights in cabins and elsewhere, until March, when, for want of food and sufficient clothing, his feet having been frost bitten, he was obliged to give in. He returned one snowy afternoon, slipped into the stable, and hid himself in the loft under the hay. His hat was discovered by his master's two sons whose conversation, which he overheard, showed that they were afraid of him. They ran to the house and told their father of his return, and he came out to the barn and urged him to come to the house and be looked after, for the entire family was really very fond of him. He was taken back to the house where his mistress, the mother of the two boys, treated him most kindly. Indeed, he said, they all wept over his pitiable condition. His feet were finally, but only after careful nursing for several months, in shape to permit him to resume his usual duties. He promised that he would not commit the same offence again, provided, however, no "po'h white trash" attempted again to whip him. He apologized to the overseer, and the two agreed that there would be no further trouble. But a few weeks afterward he went to his master and told him he was very sorry it was not possible for him to get along with that overseer and asked that his master sell him to a near-by planter, who had agreed to give him better treatment. This time it would appear that he and the master came very near the "parting of the ways." This seems strange, I know, but it was not infrequent that slaves of the more intelligent type would make definite arrangements with some near or distant planter to buy them; thus slaves very often picked their own masters. But in this case Mr. Crowder made it plain to him that they could get along; that he was unwilling to sell him; that he belonged especially to his mistress and that she depended on him. My father insisted, however, that the overseer be discharged. Whether his attitude in this case produced the desired result my father did not know, but in any case within a few weeks the objectionable overseer left and a new overseer took his place, who established better relations, not only as between himself and my father, but with the other slaves as well, in consequence of which the master got better and more efficient service with very much less friction.

From that time forward my father lived pleasantly on the Crowder plantation, neither he nor the master nor the overseer breaking their mutual promise—my father's being that he would not fight again unless someone attempted to whip him; and the overseer's, that he would not attempt to whip him. My father used to say that one man could not chastise another, although two men might fight and one might get the better of the other. That idea was very strong in his mind.

When the Civil War broke out my father went with Mrs. Crowder's brother—Captain Womack of Cumberland County, Virginia, who was afterward Colonel Womack—into the fray as his "body servant." I think they would say "valet" to-day. He was with him during the first three years of that bitter struggle, suffering all the privations and hardships so familiar to those who know what the Southern Army endured.

One experience he used often to relate was that near Petersburg he accidentally got within the Union lines and was told that he might remain with the Yankees if he so desired; but he told them that he could not do so at the time because he had given his definite promise that he would stand by Colonel Womack until the war was over. He could not break his promise. He had also sworn to see to it, so far as he could, that no harm came to his master and he felt that he would remain true to that pledge so long as Colonel Womack was equally true to his promises to him. I am told that the friendship between the two men, one black, one white, was very strong; that nothing ever separated them save Colonel Womack's death which, as I recall my father's account of it, occurred in one of the famous charges near Petersburg.

When the war was over my father "hired himself" to the Crowders, where he remained until Christmas of 1866 when he married my mother, Emily Brown. They were married in the old plantation house of the Hillmans of Amelia County. The Hillmans, as I recall, were Scottish Presbyterians and like many other Southerners, had lost everything during the war except their name and honour and the pride of aristocratic ancestry.

My mother, like her own mother, was a woman of very strong character in many ways, very much like my father. Among my early recollections is the fact that my mother frequently, after working in the field all day, would hurry us through the evening meal in order to get the cabin ready for the night school which met regularly in our simple home. I recall now the eagerness with which some twenty-five or thirty men and women struggled with their lessons, trying to learn to read and write while I was supposed to be asleep in my trundle bed, to which I had been hurried to make room for this little band of anxious, aspiring ex-slaves, some of whom came as far as six miles in order to take advantage of this rare opportunity which but a few years before had been denied them. The teacher of this night school was my mother's brother, who, in spite of the penalties attached, had learned to read and write from his young master, picking up here and there snatches of information while they played and worked together, ofttimes without the young master's realizing the gravity of his actions. All this took place but a few years after the close of the war and before any schools had been established for coloured or white children in that section. My mother was one of the most enthusiastic of the students, while my father, who was much older than my mother, although giving his unqualified approval and encouragement to the school, sat by and listened and once in a while in a mischievous mood threw in an ejaculation which upset the order and dignity of the school, much to the embarrassment and annoyance of the teacher and, I fear, sometimes to the indignation of the more serious-minded students, especially my mother.

Thinking of the experiences through which my ancestors passed, along with thousands of other slaves, in their contact with the white people of America, I have often felt that somehow in spite of the hardships and oppression which they suffered—that in the providence of God, the Negro, when all is summed up dispassionately, has come through the ordeal with much to his credit, and with a great many advantages over his condition when he entered the relationship. The white man, on the other hand, has reaped certain disadvantages from which the whole country still suffers and from which it will probably take several generations to recover completely.

Oath of Afro-American Youth

Kelly Miller

I will never bring disgrace upon my race by any unworthy deed or dishonorable act. I will live a clean, decent, manly life; and will ever respect and defend the virtue and honor of womanhood; I will uphold and obey the just laws of my country and of the community in which I live, and will encourage others to do likewise; I will not allow prejudice, injustice, insult or outrage to cower my spirit or sour my soul; but will ever preserve the inner freedom of heart and conscience; I will not allow myself to be overcome of evil, but will strive to overcome evil with good; I will endeavor to develop and exert the best powers within me for my own personal improvement, and will strive unceasingly to quicken the sense of racial duty and responsibility; I will in all these ways aim to uplift my race so that, to everyone bound to it by ties of blood, it shall become a bond of ennoblement and not a byword of reproach.

The Negro Race

Charles W. Anderson

As a race, we have done much, but we must not forget how much more there is still to do. To some extent we have been given opportunity, but we must not cease to remember that no race can be given relative rank—it must win equality of rating for itself. Hence, we must not only acquire education, but character as well. It is not only necessary that we should speak well, but it is more necessary that we should speak the truth.

A Mere Matter of the Feelings
By John Branner

I was born in the South "fo' de wah," and as my parents were slave holders, I grew up among the negroes. To me they seemed vastly more interesting and more human than white folks. During my early childhood negro girls or negro women were my nurses and keepers all day long and it required a lot of parental authority and something else that I decline to name, to keep me away from their cabins at night. I remember most vividly one particular night when I was called in from a negro cabin and brought to judgment in the presence of the assembled family. After a solemn lecture by my mother, and after she evidently thought I must be under conviction of sin, she asked if I thought the negroes were more interesting and better company than the white folks. In my innocence I replied meekly, "Yes, ma'am!" Thereafter my pursuit of happiness was interfered with in various ways, but I still managed to slip through the picket lines occasionally, and to sit for a few blissful minutes in the pile of pine knots at the corner of the fireplace in a negro cabin that was presided over by an old man and or old woman.

The conversation at such times and in such places—at least in so far as it impressed me—was always easily understood, and it was always full of dramatic interest. Even the theological instruction that I received from the negroes was realistic, cleancut, and convincing, thought it must be confessed that it was on the whole rather whimsical and only remotely related to orthodox teachings.

I recall the fact too that my questions on religious subjects were almost always answered without any hesitation, and not infrequently the answers were so clinched that serious doubt was quite impossible.

It was in these negro cabins that I first heard many of the folk-lore stories published later by Joel Chandler Harris, and a lot more besides.

Among the dearest of the old negro friends who met so satisfactorily the requirements of my childish imagination were Aunt Ellen, Uncle Peter, and Aunt Sarah or Aunt

Say as we called her. When I got big enough to wield a hoe, the hoe was place in my hands and I was required to wield it, and to keep up in the corn field with negro boys of my own age; and as we small boys were usually under the immediate supervision of a grown person, I usually managed to get one of these imaginative theological elders for my sponsor. And it was in the long corn rows along the bottoms of the French-broad river that I heard from one of the old negroes these and many other stories that have not partly or entirely escaped my memory.

It is not strange that, under the circumstances, slavery seemed to me a natural and happy state of human existence.

Then came the civil war and after that the former slaves were taken in hand by political organizations and by the fishers in the muddy waters of the times. They were inveigled away from their former homes and friends, and finally left to the waves and winds of fate like so much flotsam and jetsam of the war.

Meanwhile I had been sent to school away from home. It was, I believe, in the summer of 1867 that I returned home for a short visit, and on inquiring about our former slaves I heard that Aunt Ellen lived about eight miles away, and that she had sent word to me to be sure to come to see her when I was home on a visit. And of course I went.

I found Aunt Ellen in a state of poverty and wretchedness that went to my heart. But she had for me a good dinner of corn bread and bacon and greens, and she told me all her domestic troubles, of which she had a choice assortment. She had a drunken loafer for a husband, and a house full of children in various stages of nakedness and dirt, and growing up in shiftlessness with all the accompaniments of such conditions. Her health was not good, but she had to work hard "whedder or no," early and late, to keep the family together and alive. To me it was a sad, sad story. It seemed to me that the contrast between her condition as a slave and her condition as a free woman was an overwhelming and unanswerable argument in favor of slavery. Besides I had been living in the midst of that sort of arguments ever since the slaves had been freed. And I told her what I thought, or supposed I thought, in some such words as these: "Aunt

Allen, you were better off as a slave than you are now. You had a better house to live in, better food to eat, and better clothes to wear, and no doctor's bills to pay. You never had to worry about providing for your family, because you knew that father and mother would attend to that. If you got sick you had a doctor to look after you, and you had no bills to pay. Don't you think you were better off as a slave?"

And this is what Aunt Ellen replied: "De Lawd bless yo' soul, chile, dat's a fac'; hit's jes lak you ben a sayin'. I knows I had mo' to eat an' mo' to wear, an' a better house to live in, an' all o' dem things, an' you all was mighty good to me; an' I didn have none o' dese here doctah's bills to pay. But Law', honey, after all, dah's de feelin's!"

From that day to this I have had no more to say in favor of human slavery.

53710524R00167

Made in the USA
Columbia, SC
19 March 2019